The Story of the Rome, Watertown, and Ogdensburg Railroad

Edward Hungerford

Alpha Editions

This edition published in 2024

ISBN : 9789362998910

Design and Setting By
Alpha Editions
www.alphaedis.com
Email - info@alphaedis.com

As per information held with us this book is in Public Domain.
This book is a reproduction of an important historical work. Alpha Editions uses the best technology to reproduce historical work in the same manner it was first published to preserve its original nature. Any marks or number seen are left intentionally to preserve its true form.

Contents

PREFACE ....- 1 -

CHAPTER I BY WAY OF
INTRODUCTION ....- 2 -

CHAPTER II LOOKING TOWARD A
RAILROAD ....- 4 -

CHAPTER III THE COMING OF THE
WATERTOWN & ROME..- 14 -

CHAPTER IV THE POTSDAM &
WATERTOWN RAILROAD.......................................- 32 -

CHAPTER V THE FORMATION OF THE
R. W. & O. ....- 42 -

CHAPTER VI THE R. W. & O.
PROSPERS—AND EXPANDS ....- 54 -

CHAPTER VII INTO THE SLOUGH OF
DESPOND ....- 67 -

CHAPTER VIII THE UTICA & BLACK
RIVER..- 75 -

CHAPTER IX THE BRISK PARSONS'
REGIME ....- 89 -

CHAPTER X IN WHICH RAILROADS
MULTIPLY ....- 104 -

CHAPTER XI THE COMING OF THE
NEW YORK CENTRAL..- 115 -

CHAPTER XII THE END OF THE STORY ....- 125 -

APPENDIX A ....- 133 -

APPENDIX B ....- 136 -

PREFACE

SOME railroads, like some men, experience many of the ups and downs of life. They have their seasons of high prosperity, as well as those of deep depression. Such a road was the Rome, Watertown & Ogdensburgh. In its forty years of life it ran a full gamut of railroad existence. Alternately it was one of the best railroads in creation; and one of the worst.

The author within these pages has endeavored to put plain fact plainly. He has written without malice—if anything, he still feels within his heart a burst of warm sentiment for the old R. W. & O.—and with every effort toward absolute impartiality in setting down these events that now are History. He bespeaks for his little book, kindness, consideration, even forbearance. And looks forward to the day when again he may take up his pen in the scribbling of another narrative such as this. It has been a task. But it has been a task of real fascination.

E. H.

CHAPTER I
BY WAY OF INTRODUCTION

IN the late summer of 1836 the locomotive first reached Utica and a new era in the development of Central and Northern New York was begun.

For forty years before that time, however—in fact ever since the close of the War of the Revolution—there had been a steady and increasing trek of settlers into the heart of what was soon destined to become the richest as well as the most populous state of the Union. But its development was constantly retarded by the lack of proper transportation facilities. For while the valley of the Mohawk, the gradual portage just west of Rome and the way down to Oswego and Lake Ontario through Oneida Lake and its emptying waterways, formed the one natural passage in the whole United States of that day from the Atlantic seaboard to the Great Lakes and the little-known country beyond, it was by no means an easy pathway. Not even after the Western Inland Lock Navigation Company had built its first crude masonry locks in the narrow natural impasse at Little Falls, so that the bateaux of the early settlers, which made the rest of the route in comparative ease, might pass through its one very difficult bottle-neck.

It was not until the coming of the Erie Canal, there in the second decade of the nineteenth century, that the route into the heart of New York from tidewater at Albany, was rendered a reasonably safe and (for that day) comfortable affair. With the completion of the Erie Canal, in 1827, there was immediately inaugurated a fleet of packet-boats; extremely swift in their day and generation and famed for many a day thereafter for their comfortable cabins and the excellence of their meals.

But the comfort of these ancient craft should not be overrated. At the best they were but slow affairs indeed, taking three days to come from Albany, where they connected with the early steamboats upon the Hudson, up to Utica. And at the best they might operate but seven or eight months out of the year. The rest of the twelvemonth, the unlucky wight of a traveler must needs have recourse to a horse-drawn coach.

These selfsame coaches were not to be scoffed at, however. Across the central portion of New York; by relays all the way from Albany to Black Rock or Buffalo, they made a swift passage of it. And up into the great and little known North Country they sometimes made exceeding speed. That country had received its first artificial pathways at the time of the coming of the Second War with England, when it was thrust into a sudden and great strategic importance. With the direct result that important permanent highroads were at once constructed; from Utica north to the Black River country, down the water-shed of that stream, and through Watertown to Sackett's Harbor; and from Sackett's Harbor through Brownville—the county seat and for a time the military headquarters of General Jacob Brown—north to Ogdensburgh, thence east along the Canada line to Plattsburgh upon Lake Champlain.

These military roads still remain. And beside them traces of their erstwhile glory. Usually these last in the form of ancient taverns—most often built of limestone, the stone whitened to a marblelike color by the passing of a hundred years, save where loving vines and ivy have clambered over their surfaces. You may see them to-day all the way from Utica to Sackett's Harbor; and, in turn, from Sackett's Harbor north and east to Plattsburgh once again. But none more sad nor more melancholy than at Martinsburgh; once in her pride the shire-town of the county of Lewis, but now a mere hamlet of a few fine old homes and crumbling warehouses. A great fire in the early fifties ended the ambitions of Martinsburgh—in a single short hour destroyed it almost totally. And made its hated rival Lowville, two miles to its north, the county seat and chief village of the vicinage.

There was much in this North Road to remind one of its prototype, the Great North Road, which ran and still runs from London to York, far overseas. A something in its relative importance that helps to make the parallel. Whilst even the famous four-in-hands of its English predecessor might hardly hope to do better than was done on this early road of our own North Country. It is a matter of record that on February 19, 1829, and with a level fall of thirty inches of snow upon the road, the mailstage went from Utica to Sackett's Harbor, ninety-three miles, in nine hours and forty-five minutes, including thirty-nine minutes for stops, horse relays and the like. Which would not be bad time with a motor car this day.

CHAPTER II
LOOKING TOWARD A RAILROAD

THE locomotive having reached Utica—upon the completion of the Utica & Schenectady Railroad, August 2, 1836—was not to be long content to make that his western stopping point. The fever of railroad building was upon Central New York. Railroads it must have; railroads it would have. But railroad building was not the quick and comparatively simple thing then that it is to-day. And it was not until nearly four years after he had first poked his head into Utica that the iron horse first thrust his nose into Syracuse, fifty-three miles further west. In fact the railroad from this last point to Auburn already had been completed more than a twelvemonth and but fifteen months later trains would be running all the way from Syracuse to Rochester; with but a single change of cars, at Auburn.

Upon the heels of this pioneer chain of railroads—a little later to achieve distinction as the New York Central—came the building of a railroad to the highly prosperous Lake Ontario port of Oswego—the earliest of all white settlements upon the Great Lakes.

At first it was planned that this railroad to the shores of Ontario should deflect from the Utica & Syracuse Railroad—whose completion had followed so closely upon the heels of the line between Schenectady and Utica—near Rome, and after crossing Wood Creek and Fish Creek, should follow the north shore of Oneida Lake and then down the valley of the Oswego River. Oswego is but 185 miles from Lewiston by water and it was then estimated that it could be reached in twenty-four or twenty-five hours from New York by this combined rail and water route.

Eventually however the pioneer line to Oswego was built out of Syracuse, known at first as the Oswego and Syracuse Railroad; it afterwards became a part of the Syracuse, Binghamton and New York and as a part of that line eventually was merged, in 1872, into the Delaware, Lackawanna & Western Railroad, which continues to operate it. This line of road led from the original Syracuse station, between Salina and Warren Streets straight to the waterside at Oswego harbor. There it made several boat connections; the most important of these, the fleet of mail and passenger craft operated by the one-time Ontario & St. Lawrence Steamboat Company.

The steamers of this once famous line played no small part in the development of the North Country. They operated through six or seven months of the year, as a direct service between Lewiston which had at that time highway and then later rail connection with Niagara Falls and Buffalo, through Ogdensburgh, toward which, as we shall see in good time, the Northern Railroad was being builded, close to the Canada line from Lake Champlain and the Central Vermont Railroad at St. Albans as an outlet between Northern New England and the water-borne traffic of the Great Lakes. The steamers of this line, whose names, as well as the names of their captains, were once household words in the North Country were:

Northerner	Captain	R. F. Child
Ontario	"	H. N. Throop
Bay State	"	J. Van Cleve
New York	"	————
Cataract	"	R. B. Chapman
British Queen	"	Laflamme
British Empire	"	Moody

The first four of these steamers, each flying the American flag, were deservedly the best known of the fleet. The Ontario, the Bay State and the New York were built at French Creek upon the St Lawrence (now Clayton) by John Oakes; the Northerner was Oswego-built. They burned wood in the beginning, and averaged about 230 feet in length and about 900 tons burthen. There were in the fleet one or two other less consequential boats, among them the Rochester, which plied between Lewiston and Hamilton, in the then Canada West, as a connecting steamer with the main line. The steamer Niagara, Captain A. D. Kilby, left Oswego each Monday, Wednesday and Friday evening at eight, passing Rochester the next morning and arriving at Toronto at four p. m. Returning she would leave Toronto on the alternating days at 8:00 p. m., pass Rochester at 5:30 a. m. and arrive at Oswego at 10:00 a. m., in full time to connect with the Oswego & Syracuse R. R. train for Syracuse, and by connection, to Albany and the Hudson River steamers for New York. A little later Captain John S. Warner, of Henderson Harbor, was the Master of the Niagara.

The "line boats," as the larger craft were known, also connected with these through trains. In the morning they did not depart until after the arrival of the train from Syracuse. In detail their schedule by 1850 was as follows:

Lv. Lewiston	4 p.m.	Lv. Montreal	9 a.m.
" Rochester	10 p.m.	" Ogdensburgh	8 a.m.

" Oswego	9 a.m.	" Kingston	4 p.m.
" Sackett's Harbor	12 m.	" Sackett's Harbor	9 p.m.
" Ogdensburgh	7 a.m.	" Oswego	10 a.m.
Ar. Montreal	6 p.m.	" Rochester	6 p.m.
		Ar. Lewiston	4 a.m.

Here for many years, before the coming of the railroad, was an agreeable way of travel into Northern New York. These steamers, even with thirty foot paddle-wheels, were not fast; on the contrary they were extremely slow. Neither were they gaudy craft, as one might find in other parts of the land. But their rates of fare were very low and their meals, which like the berths, were included in the cost of the passage ticket, had a wide reputation for excellence. Until the coming of the railroad into Northern New York, the line prospered exceedingly. Indeed, for a considerable time thereafter it endeavored to compete against the railroad—but with a sense of growing hopelessness. And eventually these once famous steamers having grown both old and obsolete, the line was abandoned.

A rival line upon the north edge of Lake Ontario, the Richelieu & Ontario, continued to prosper for many years, however, after the coming of the railroad. Its steamers—the Corsican, the Caspian, the Algerian, the Spartan, the Corinthian and the Passport best known, perhaps, amongst them—ran from Hamilton, touching at Toronto, Kingston, Clayton, Alexandria Bay, Prescott and Cornwall, through to Montreal, where connections were made in turn for lower river ports. The last of these boats continued in operation upon the St. Lawrence until within twenty years or thereabouts ago.

It is worthy of note that the completion in 1829 of the first Welland Canal began to turn a really huge tide of traffic from Lake Erie into Lake Ontario, and for two decades this steadily increased. In 1850 Ontario bore some 400,000 tons of freight upon its bosom, yet in the following year this had increased to nearly 700,000 tons, valued at more than thirty millions of dollars. In 1853 a tonnage mark of more than a million was passed and the Lake then achieved an activity that it has not known since. In that year the Watertown & Rome Railroad began its really active operations and the traffic of Ontario to dwindle in consequence. Whilst the cross-St. Lawrence ferry at Cape Vincent, the first northern terminal of the Rome road, began to assume an importance that it was not to lose for nearly forty years.

Steamboat travel was hardly to be relied upon in a country which suffers so rigorous a winter climate as that of Northern New York. And highway travel in the bitter months between November and April was hardly better. A railroad was the thing; and a railroad the North Country must have. The agitation grew for a direct line at least between Watertown, already coming into importance as a manufacturing center of much diversity of product, to the Erie Canal and the chain of separate growing railroads, that by the end of 1844, stretched as a continuous line of rails all the way from Albany—and by way of the Western and the Boston & Worcester Railroads (to-day the Boston and Albany) all the way from Boston itself—to Buffalo and Niagara Falls. Prosperity already was upon the North Country. It was laying the foundations of its future wealth. It was ordained that a railroad should be given it. The problem was just how and where that railroad should be built. After a brief but bitter fight between Rome and Utica for the honor of being the chief terminal of this railroad up into the North Country, Rome was chosen; as far back as 1832. Yet it was not until sixteen years later that the construction of the Watertown & Rome Railroad, the pioneer road of Northern New York, was actually begun. And had been preceded by a mighty and almost continuous legislative battle in the old Capitol at Albany ... of which more in another chapter.

In the meantime other railroads had been projected into the North Country. The real pioneer among all of these was the Northern Railroad, which was projected to run due west from Rouse's Point to Ogdensburgh, just above the head of the highest of the rapids of the St. Lawrence and so at that time at the foot of the easy navigation of Ontario, and, by way of the Welland Canal, of the entire chain of Great Lakes.

The preliminary discussions which finally led to the construction of this important early line also went as far back as 1829. Finally a meeting was called (at Montpelier, Vt., on February 17, 1830) to seriously consider the building of a railroad across the Northern Tier of New York counties, from Rouse's Point, upon Lake Champlain, to Ogdensburgh, upon the St. Lawrence. The promoters of the plan averred that trains might be operated over the proposed line at fifteen miles an hour, that the entire journey from Boston to Ogdensburgh might be accomplished in thirty-five hours. There were, of course, many wise men who shook their heads at the rashness of such prediction. But the idea fascinated them none the less; and twenty-eight days later a similar meeting to that at Montpelier was held at Ogdensburgh, to be followed a year later by one at Malone.

So was the idea born. It grew, although very slowly. Communication itself in the North Country was slow in those days, even though the fine military road from Sackett's Harbor through Ogdensburgh to Plattsburgh was a tolerable artery of travel most of the year. Money also was slow. And men, over enterprises so extremely new and so untried as railroads, most diffident. For it must be remembered that when the promoters of the Northern Railroad first made that outrageous promise of going from Boston to Ogdensburgh in thirty-five hours, at fifteen miles an hour, the railroad in the United States was barely born. The first locomotive—the Stourbridge Lion, at Honesdale, Penn.—had been operated less than a twelvemonth before. In the entire United States there were less than twenty-three miles of railroad in operation. So wonder it not that the plan for the Northern Railroad grew very slowly indeed; that it did not reach incorporation until fourteen long years afterward, when the Legislature of New York authorized David C. Judson and Joseph Barnes, of St. Lawrence County, S. C. Wead, of Franklin County and others as commissioners to receive and distribute stock of the Northern Railroad; $2,000,000 all told, divided into shares of $50 each. The date of the formal incorporation of the road was May 14, 1845. Its organization was not accomplished, however, until June, 1845, when the first meeting was held in the then village of Ogdensburgh, and the following officers elected:

President, GEORGE PARISH, Ogdensburgh

Treasurer, S. S. WALLEY

Secretary, JAMES G. HOPKINS

Chief Engineer, COL. CHARLES L. SCHLATTER

Directors

J. Leslie Russell, Canton	Anthony C. Brown, Ogdensburgh
Charles Paine, Northfield, Vt.	Isaac Spalding, Nashua, N. H.
Hiram Horton, Malone	Lawrence Myers, Plattsburgh
S. F. Belknap, Windsor, Vt.	Abbot Lawrence, Boston
J. Wiley Edmonds, Boston	T. P. Chandler, Boston
Benjamin Reed, Boston	S. S. Lewis, Boston

Soon after the organization of the company, T. P. Chandler succeeded Mr. Parish (who was for many years easily the most prominent citizen of Ogdensburgh) as President, and steps were taken toward the immediate construction of the line. After the inevitable preliminary contentions as to the exact route to be followed, James Hayward made the complete surveys of the line as it exists at present, while Colonel Schlatter, its chief engineer and for a number of years its superintendent as well, prepared to build it. Actual construction was begun in March, 1848, in the deep cutting just east of Ogdensburgh. At the same time grading and the laying of rail began at the east end of the road—at Rouse's Point at the foot of Lake

Champlain—with the result that in the fall of 1848 trains were in regular operation between Rouse's Point and Centreville. A year later the road had been extended to Ellenburgh; in June, 1850, to Chateaugay. On October 1, 1850, trains ran into Malone. A month later it was finished and open for its entire length of 117 miles. Its cost, including its equipment and fixtures, was then placed at $5,022,121.31.

It is not within the province of this little book to set down in detail the somewhat checkered career of the Northern Railroad. It started with large ambitions—even before its incorporation, James G. Hopkins, who afterwards became its Secretary, traveled through the Northern Tier and expatiated upon its future possibilities in a widely circulated little pamphlet. It was a road built for a large traffic. So sure were its promoters of this forthcoming business that they placed its track upon the side of the right-of-way, rather than in the middle of it, in order that it would not have to be moved when it came time to double-track the road.

The road was never double-tracked. For some years it prospered—very well. It made a direct connection between the large lake steamers at the foot of navigation at Ogdensburgh—it will be remembered that Ogdensburgh is just above the swift-running and always dangerous rapids of the St. Lawrence—and the important port of Boston. The completion of the line was followed almost immediately by the construction of a long bridge across the foot of Lake Champlain which brought it into direct connection with the rails of the Central Vermont at St. Albans—and so in active touch with all of the New England lines.

The ambitious hopes of the promoters of the Northern took shape not only in the construction of the stone shops and the large covered depot at Malone (built in 1850 by W. A. Wheeler—afterwards not only President of the property, but Vice-President of the United States—it still stands in active service) but in the building of 4000 feet of wharfage and elaborate warehouses and other terminal structures upon the river bank at Ogdensburgh. The most of these also still stand—memorials of the large scale upon which the road originally was designed.

Gradually, however, its strength faded. Other rail routes, more direct and otherwise more advantageous, came to combat it. Fewer and still fewer steamers came to its Ogdensburgh docks—at the best it was a seasonal business; the St. Lawrence is thoroughly frozen and out of use for about five months out of each year. The steamers of the upper Lakes outgrew in size the locks of the Welland Canal and so made for Buffalo—in increasing numbers. The Northern Railroad entered upon difficulties, to put it mildly. It was reorganized and reorganized; it became the Ogdensburgh Railroad, then the Ogdensburgh & Lake Champlain, then a branch of the Central Vermont and then upon the partial dismemberment of that historic property, a branch of the Rutland Railroad. As such it still continues with a moderate degree of success. In any narrative of the development of transport in the North Country it must be forever regarded, however, as a genuine pioneer among its railroads.

One other route was seriously projected from the eastern end of the state into the North Country—the Sackett's Harbor and Saratoga Railroad Co. which was chartered April 10, 1848. After desperate efforts to build a railroad through the vast fastnesses of the North Woods—then a terra incognito, almost impenetrable—and the expenditure of very considerable sums of money, both in surveys and in actual construction, this enterprise was finally abandoned. Yet one to-day can still see traces of it across the forest. In the neighborhood of Beaver Falls, they become most definite; a long cutting and an embankment reaching from it, a melancholy reminder of a mighty human endeavor of just seventy years ago. If this route had ever been completed, Watertown to-day would enjoy direct rail communication with Boston, although not reaching within a dozen miles of Albany. The Fitchburg, which always sought, but vainly, to make itself an effective competitor of the powerful Boston & Albany, built itself through to Saratoga Springs, largely in hopes that some day the line through the forest to Sackett's Harbor would be completed. It was a vain hope. The faintest chance of that line ever being built was quite gone. A quarter of a century later the Fitchburg thrust another branch off from its Saratoga line to reach the ambitious new West Shore at Rotterdam Junction. That hope also faded. And the Fitchburg, now an important division of the Boston & Maine, despite its direct route and short mileage through the Hoosac Tunnel, became forever a secondary route across the state of Massachusetts.

The reports of the prospecting parties of the Sackett's Harbor & Saratoga form a pleasing picture of the Northern New York at the beginning of the fifties. The company had been definitely formed with its chief offices at 80 Wall Street, New York, and the following officers and directors:

    President, WILLIAM COVENTRY H. WADDELL, New York

   Supt. of Operations, GEN. S. P. LYMAN, New York

     Treasurer, HENRY STANTON, New York

Secretary, SAMUEL ELLIS, Boston

Counsel, SAMUEL BEARDSLEY, Utica

Consulting Engineer, JOHN B. MILLS, New York

Directors

Charles E. Clarke, Great Bend	P. Somerville Stewart, Carthage
Lyman R. Lyon, Lyons Falls	E. G. Merrick, French Creek
Robert Speir, West Milton	James M. Marvin, Saratoga
John R. Thurman, Chester	Anson Thomas, Utica
Zadock Pratt, Prattsville	Otis Clapp, Boston
Wm. Coventry H. Waddell, New York	Gen. S. P. Lyman, Utica

Henry Stanton, New York

Mr. A. F. Edwards received his appointment as Chief Engineer of the company on March 10, 1852, and soon afterwards entered upon a detailed reconnoissance of the territory embraced within its charter. He examined closely into its mineral and timber resources and gave great attention to its future agricultural and industrial possibilities. In the early part of his report he says:

"In the latter part of September, 1852, I left Saratoga for the Racket (Racquette) Lake, via Utica. On my way I noticed on the Mohawk that there had been frost, and as I rode along in the stage from Utica to Boonville, I saw that the frost had bitten quite sharply the squash vines and the potatoes, the leaves having become quite black; but judge my surprise, when three days later on visiting the settlement of the Racket, I found the beans, cucumber vines, potatoes, &c., as fresh as in midsummer."

His examination of the territory completed, Mr. Edwards began the rough location of the line of the new railroad. From Saratoga it passed westerly to the valley of the Kayaderosseras, in the town of Greenfield, thence north through Greenfield Center, South Corinth and through the "Antonio Notch" in the town of Corinth to the Sacondaga valley, up which it proceeded to the village of Conklingville, easterly through Huntsville and Northville, through the town of Hope to "the Forks." From there it went up the east branch of the Sacondaga, through Wells and Gilman to the isolated town of Lake Pleasant. Spruce Lake and the headwaters of the Canada Creek were threaded to the summit of the line at the Canada Lakes.

The middle and the western branches of the Moose River were passed near Old Forge and the line descended the Otter Creek valley, crossing the Independence River and down the Crystal Creek through and near Dayansville and Beaver Falls to Carthage where for the first time it would touch the Black River.

From Carthage to Watertown it was planned that it would closely follow the Black River valley, crossing the river three times, and leaving it at Watertown for a straight run across the flats to Sackett's Harbor; along the route of the already abandoned canal which Elisha Camp and a group of associates had built in 1822 and had left to its fate in 1832; in fact almost precisely upon the line of the present Sackett's Harbor branch of the New York Central. At the Harbor great terminal developments were planned; an inner harbor in the village and an outer one of considerable magnitude at Horse Island.

From Carthage a branch line was projected to French Creek, now the busy summer village of Clayton. The route was to diverge from the main line about one mile west of Great Bend thence running in a tangent to the Indian River, about a mile and one-half east of Evan's Mills, where after crossing that stream upon a bridge of two spans and at a height of sixty feet would recross it two miles further on and then run in an almost straight line to Clayton. Here a very elaborate harbor improvement was planned, with a loop track and almost continuous docks to encircle the compact peninsula upon which the village is built.

"At French Creek on a clear day," says Mr. Edwards, "the roofs of the buildings at Kingston, across the St. Lawrence, can be seen with the naked eye. All the steamers and sail vessels, up and down the river and lake, pass this place and when the Grand Trunk Railroad is completed, it will be as convenient a point as can be found to connect with the same."

All the while he waxes most enthusiastic about the future possibilities of Northern New York, particularly the westerly counties of it. He calls attention to the thriving villages of Turin, Martinsburgh, Lowville, Denmark, Lyonsdale (I am leaving the older names as he gives them in his report) and Dayansville, in the Black River valley.

"In the wealthy county of Jefferson," he adds, "are the towns of Carthage, Great Bend, Felt's Mills, Lockport (now Black River), Brownville and Dexter, with Watertown, its county seat, well located for a manufacturing city, having ample water power, at the same time surrounded by a country rich in its soil and highly cultivated to meet the wants of the operatives. Watertown contains about 10,000 inhabitants and is the most modern, city-like built, inland town in the Union, containing about 100 stores, five banks, cotton and woolen factories, six large flouring mills, machine shops, furnaces, paper mills, and innumerable other branches of business, with many first class hotels, among which the 'Woodruff House' may be justly called the Metropolitan of Western New York."

In that early day, more than $795,000 had been invested in manufacturing enterprises along the Black River, at Watertown and below. The territory was a fine traffic plum for any railroad project. It seems a pity that after all the ambitious dreams of the Sackett's Harbor & Saratoga and the very considerable expenditures that were made upon its right-of-way, that it was to be doomed to die without ever having operated a single through train. The nineteen or twenty miles of its line that were put down, north and west from Saratoga Springs, long since lost their separate identity as a branch of the Delaware & Hudson system.

CHAPTER III
THE COMING OF THE WATERTOWN & ROME

THE first successful transportation venture of the North Country was still ahead of it. The efforts of these patient souls, who struggled so hard to establish the Northern Railroad as an entrance to the six counties from the east, were being echoed by those who strove to gain a rail entrance into it from the south. Long ago in this narrative we saw how as far back as 1836 the locomotive first entered Utica. Six or seven years later there was a continuous chain of railroads from Albany to Buffalo—precursors of the present New York Central—and ambitious plans for building feeder lines to them from surrounding territory, both to the north and to the south. The early Oswego & Syracuse Railroad was typical of these.

Of all these plans none was more ambitious, however, than that which sought to build a line from Rome into the heart of the rich county of Jefferson, the lower valley of the Black River and the St. Lawrence River at almost the very point where Lake Ontario debouches into it. The scheme for this road, in actuality, antedated the coming of the locomotive into Utica by four years, for it was in 1832—upon the 17th day of April in that year—that the Watertown & Rome Railroad was first incorporated and Henry H. Coffeen, Edmund Kirby, Orville Hungerford and William Smith of Jefferson County, Hiram Hubbell, Caleb Carr, Benjamin H. Wright and Elisha Hart, of Oswego, and Jesse Armstrong, Alvah Sheldon, Artemas Trowbridge and Seth D. Roberts, of Oneida, named by the Legislature as commissioners to promote the enterprise. Later George C. Sherman, of Watertown, was added to these commissioners. The act provided that the road should be begun within three years and completed within five. Its capital stock was fixed at $1,000,000, divided into shares of $100 each.

The commercial audacity, the business daring of these men of the North Country in even seeking to establish so huge an enterprise in those early days of its settlement is hard to realize in this day, when our transport has come to be so facile and easily understood a thing. Their courage was the courage of mental giants. The railroad was less than three years established in the United States; in the entire world less than five. Yet they sought to bring into Northern New York, there at the beginning of the third decade of the nineteenth century, hardly emerged from primeval forest, the highway of iron rail, that even so highly a developed civilization as that of England was receiving with great caution and uncertainty.

These men of the North Country had not alone courage, but vision; not alone vision, but perseverance. Their railroad once born, even though as a trembling thing that for years existed upon paper only, was not permitted to die. It could not die. And that it should live the pioneers of Jefferson and Oswego rode long miles over unspeakably bad roads with determination in their hearts.

The act that established the Watertown & Rome Railroad was never permitted to expire. It was revived; again and again and again—in 1837, in 1845, and again in 1847. It is related how night after night William Smith and Clarke Rice used to sit in an upper room of a house on Factory Street in Watertown—then as now, the shire-town of Jefferson—and exhibit to callers a model of a tiny train running upon a little track. Factory Street was then one of the most attractive residence streets of Watertown. The irony of fate was yet to transfer it into a rather grimy artery of commerce—by the single process of the building of the main line of the Potsdam & Watertown Railroad throughout its entire length.

These men, and others, kept the project alive. William Dewey was one of its most enthusiastic proponents. As the result of a meeting held at Pulaski on June 27, 1836, he had been chosen to survey a line from Watertown to Rome—through Pulaski. With the aid of Robert F. Livingston and James Roberts, this was accomplished in the fall of 1836. Soon after Dewey issued two thousand copies of a small thirty-two page pamphlet, entitled Suggestions Urging the Construction of a Railroad from Rome to Watertown. It was a potent factor in advocating the new enterprise; so potent, in fact, that Cape Vincent, alarmed at not being included in all of these plans, held a mass-meeting which was followed by the incorporation of the Watertown & Cape Vincent Railroad, with a modest capitalization of but $50,000. Surveys followed, and the immediate result of this step was to include the present Cape Vincent branch in all the plans for the construction of the original Watertown & Rome Railroad.

These plans, as we have just seen, did not move rapidly. It is possible that the handicap of the great distances of the North Country might have been overcome had it not been that 1837 was destined as the year of the first great financial crash that the United States had ever known. The northern counties of New York were by no means immune from the severe effects of that disaster. Money was tight. The future looked dark. But the two gentlemen of Watertown kept their little train going there in the small room on Factory Street. Faith in any time or place is a superb thing. In business it is a very real asset indeed. And the faith of Clarke Rice and William Smith was reflected in the courage of Dewey, who would not let the new road die.

To keep it alive he rode up and down the proposed route on horseback, summer and winter, urging its great necessity.

Out of that faith came large action once again. Railroad meetings began to multiply in the North Country; the success of similar enterprises, not only in New York State, but elsewhere within the Union, was related to them. Finally there came one big meeting, on a very cold 10th of February in 1847, in the old Universalist Church at Watertown. All Watertown came to it; out of it grew a definite railroad.

Yet it grew very slowly. In the files of the old Northern State Journal, of Watertown, and under the date of March 29, 1848, I find an irritated editorial reference to the continual delays in the building of the road. Under the heading "Our Railroad," the Journal describes a railroad meeting held in the Jefferson County Court House a few days before and goes on to say:

"... Seldom has any meeting been held in this county where more unanimity and enthusiastic devotion to a great public object have been displayed, than was evidenced in the character and conduct of the assemblage that filled the Court House.... Go ahead, and that immediately, was the ruling motto in the speeches and resolutions and the whole meeting sympathized in the sentiment. And indeed, it is time to go ahead. It is now about sixteen years since a charter was first obtained and yet the first blow is not struck. No excuse for further delay will be received. None will be needed. We understand that measures have already been taken to expend in season the amount necessary to secure the charter—to call in the first installment of five per cent—to organize and put upon the line the requisite number of engineers and surveyors—and to hold an election for a new Board of Directors.

"We trust that none but efficient men, firm friends of the Railroad, will be put in the Direction. The Stockholders should look to this and vote for no man that they do not know to be warmly in favor of an active prosecution of the work to an early completion. This subject has been so long before the community that every man's sentiments are known, and it would be folly to expose the road to defeat now by not being careful in the selection. With a Board of Directors such as can be found, the autumn of 1849 should be signalized by the opening of the entire road from the Cape to Rome. It can be done and it should be done. The road being a great good the sooner we enjoy it the better."

So it was that upon the sixth day of the following April the actual organization of the Watertown & Rome Railroad was accomplished at the American Hotel, in Watertown, and an emissary despatched to Albany, who succeeded on April 28th in having the original Act for the construction of the line extended, for a final time. It also provided for the increase of the capitalization from $1,000,000 to $1,500,000—in order that the new road, once built, could be properly equipped with iron rail, weighing at least fifty-six pounds to the yard. It was not difficult by that time to sell the additional stock in the company. The missionary work—today we would call it propaganda—of its first promoters really had been a most thorough job.

ORVILLE HUNGERFORD
First President of the Watertown & Rome Railroad.

The original officers of the Watertown & Rome Railroad were:

President, ORVILLE HUNGERFORD, Watertown

Secretary, CLARKE RICE, Watertown

Treasurer, O. V. BRAINARD, Watertown

Superintendent, R. B. DOXTATER, Watertown

Directors

S. N. Dexter, New York   Clarke Rice, Watertown

William C. Pierrepont, Brooklyn	Robert B. Doxtater, New York
John H. Whipple, New York	Orville Hungerford, Watertown
Norris M. Woodruff, Watertown	William Smith, Watertown
Samuel Buckley, Watertown	Edmund Kirby, Brownville
Jerre Carrier, Cape Vincent	Theophilus Peugnet, Cape Vincent

The summer of 1847 was spent chiefly in perfecting the organization and financial plans of the new road, in eliminating a certain opposition to it within its own ranks and in strengthening its morale. At the initial meeting of the Board of Directors, William Smith had been allowed two dollars a day for soliciting subscriptions while Messrs. Hungerford, Pierrepont, Doxtater and Dexter were appointed a committee to go to New York and Boston for the same purpose. A campaign fund of $500 was allotted for this entire purpose.

The question of finances was always a delicate and a difficult one. In the minutes of the Board for May 10, 1848, I find that the question of where the road should bank its funds had been a vexed one, indeed. It was then settled by dividing the amount into twentieths, of which the Jefferson County Bank should have eight, the Black River, four, Hungerford's, three, the Bank of Watertown, three, and Wooster Sherman's two.

Gradually these funds accumulated. The subscriptions had been solicited upon a partial payment basis and these initial payments of five and ten percent were providing the money for the expenses of organization and careful survey. This last was accomplished in the summer of 1848, by Isaac W. Crane, who had been engaged as Chief Engineer of the property at $2500 a year. Mr. Crane made careful resurveys of the route—omitting Pulaski this time; to the very great distress of that village—and estimated the complete cost of the road at about $1,250,000. It is interesting to note that its actual cost, when completed, was $1,957,992.

In that same summer, Mr. Brainard retired as Treasurer of the company and was succeeded by Daniel Lee, of Watertown, whose annual compensation was fixed at $800. Later, Mr. Lee increased this, by taking upon his shoulders the similar post of the Potsdam & Watertown. The infant Watertown & Rome found need of offices for itself. It engaged quarters over Tubbs' Hat Store, which modestly it named The Railroad Rooms and there it was burned out in the great fire of Watertown, May 13, 1849.

All of these were indeed busy months of preparation. There were locomotives to be ordered. Four second-hand engines, as we shall see in a moment, were bought at once in New England, but the old engine Cayuga, which the Schenectady & Utica had offered the Rome road at a bargain-counter price of $2500 finally was refused. Negotiations were then begun with the Taunton Locomotive Works for the construction of engines which would be quite the equal of any turned out in the land up to that time; and which were to be delivered to the company, at its terminal at Rome—at a cost of $7150 apiece. Horace W. Woodruff, of Watertown, was given the contract for building the cars for the new line; he was to be paid for them, one-third in the stock of the company and two-thirds in cash. His car-works were upon the north bank of the Black River, upon the site now occupied by the Wise Machine Company and it was necessary to haul the cars by oxen to the rails of the new road, then in the vicinity of Watertown Junction. Yet despite the fact that his works in Watertown never had a railroad siding Woodruff later attained quite a fame as a builder of sleeping-cars. His cars at one time were used almost universally upon the railroads of the Southwest.

Construction began upon the new line at Rome, obviously chosen because of the facility with which materials could be brought to that point, either by rail or by canal—although no small part of the iron for the road was finally brought across the Atlantic and up the St. Lawrence to Cape Vincent. Nat Hazeltine is credited with having turned the first bit of sod for the line. The gentle nature of the country to be traversed by the new railroad—the greater part of it upon the easy slopes at the easterly end of Lake Ontario—presented no large obstacles, either to the engineers or the contractors, these last, Messrs. Phelps, Matoon and Barnes, of Springfield, Massachusetts. The rails, as provided in the extension of the road's charter, were fifty-six pounds to the yard (to-day they are for the greater part in excess of 100) and came from the rolling-mills of Guest & Company, in Wales. The excellence of their material and their workmanship is evidenced by the fact that they continued in service for many years, without a single instance of breakage. When they finally were removed it was because they were worn out and quite unfit for further service.

Construction once begun, went ahead very slowly, but unceasingly. By the fall of 1850 track was laid for about twenty-four miles north of Rome and upon September 10th of that year, a passenger service was installed between Rome and Camden. Fares were fixed at three cents a mile—later a so-called second-class, at one and one-half cents a mile was added—and a brisk business started at once.

It was not until May of the following year that the iron horse first poked his nose into the county of Jefferson. The (Watertown) Reformer announced in its issue of May 1 that year that the six miles of track already laid that spring would come into use that very week, bringing the completed line into the now forgotten hamlet of Washingtonville in the north part of Oswego county. Two weeks later, it predicted it would be in Jefferson.

Its prediction was accurately fulfilled. On the twenty-eighth day of the month, at Pierrepont Manor, this important event formally came to pass and was attended by a good-sized conclave of prominent citizens, who afterwards repaired to the home of Mr. William C. Pierrepont, not far from the depot, where refreshments were served. The rest your historian leaves to your imagination.

At that day and hour it seemed as if Pierrepont Manor was destined to become an important town. The land office of its great squire was still doing a thriving business. For Pierrepont Manor then, and for ten years afterwards, was a railroad junction, with a famous eating-house as one of its appendages. It seems that Sackett's Harbor had decided that it was not going to permit itself to be outdone in this railroad business by Cape Vincent. If the Harbor could not realize its dream of a railroad to Saratoga it might at least build one to the new Watertown & Rome road there at Pierrepont Manor, and so gain for itself a direct route to both New York and Boston. And as a fairly immediate extension, a line on to Pulaski, which might eventually reach Syracuse, was suggested.

At any rate, on May 23, 1850, the Sackett's Harbor & Ellisburgh Railroad was incorporated. Funds were quickly raised for its construction, and it was builded almost coincidently with the Watertown & Rome. Thomas Stetson, of Boston, had the contract for building the line; being paid $150,000; two-thirds in cash and one-third in its capital stock. It was completed and opened for business by the first day of January, 1853. It was not destined, however, for a long existence. From the beginning it failed to bring adequate returns—the Watertown & Rome management quite naturally favoring its own water terminal at Cape Vincent. By 1860 it was in a fearful quagmire. In November of that year, W. T. Searle, of Belleville, its President and Superintendent, wrote to the State Engineer and Surveyor at Albany, saying that the road had reorganized itself as the Sackett's Harbor, Rome & New York, and that it was going to take a new try at life. But it was a hard outlook.

"The engine used by the company," Mr. Searle wrote, "belongs to persons, who purchased it for the purpose of the operation of the road when it was known by the corporate name of the Sackett's Harbor & Ellisburgh, and has cost the corporation nothing up to the end of this year for its use. All the cars used on the road (there were only four) except the passenger-car, are in litigation, but in the possession of individuals, principally stockholders in this road, who have allowed the corporation the use of them free of expense...."

Yet despite this gloom, the little road was keeping up at least the pretense of its service. It had two trains a day; leaving Pierrepont Manor at 9:40 a. m. and 5:00 p. m. and after intermediate stops at Belleville, Henderson and Smithville reaching Sackett's Harbor at 10:45 a. m. (a connection with the down boat for Kingston and for Ogdensburgh) and at 6:30 p. m. The trains returned from the Harbor at 11:00 a. m. and 7:00 p. m.

Reorganization, the grace of a new name, failed to save this line. The Civil War broke upon the country, with it times of surpassing hardness and in 1862 it was abandoned; the following year its rails torn up forever. Yet to this day one who is even fairly acquainted with the topography of Jefferson County may trace its path quite clearly.

Here ended then, rather ignominiously to be sure, a fairly ambitious little railroad project. And while Sackett's Harbor was eventually to have rail transport service restored to it, Belleville was henceforth to be left nearly stranded—until the coming of the improved highway and the motor-propelled vehicle upon it. Yet it was Belleville that had furnished most of the inspiration and the capital for the Sackett's Harbor & Ellisburgh. And even though in its old records I find Mr. M. Loomis, of the Harbor, listed as its Treasurer, Secretary, General Freight Agent and General Ticket Agent—a regular Pooh Bah sort of a job—W. T. Searle, of Belleville, was its President and Superintendent; and A. Dickinson, of the same village, its Vice-President; George Clarke and A. J. Barney among the Directors. These men had dared much to bring the railroad to their village and failing eventually must finally have conceded much to the impotence of human endeavor.

In the summer of 1851 work upon the Watertown & Rome steadily went forward and at a swifter pace than ever before. All the way through to Cape Vincent the contractors were at work upon the new line. They were racing against time itself almost to complete the road. There were valuable mail contracts to be obtained and upon these hung much of the immediate financial success of the road.

In the spring of 1922, by a rare stroke of good fortune, the author of this book was enabled to obtain firsthand the story of the construction of the northern section of the line. At Kane, Pa., he found a venerable gentleman, Mr. Richard T. Starsmeare, who at the extremely advanced age of ninety-five years was able to tell with a marvelous clearness of the part that he, himself, had played in the construction of the line between Chaumont and Cape Vincent. With a single wave of his hand he rolled back seventy long years and told in simple fashion the story of his connection with the Watertown & Rome:

Young Starsmeare, a native of London, at the age of twenty had run away to sea. He crossed on a lumber-ship to Quebec and slowly made his way up the valley of the St. Lawrence. The year, 1850, had scarce been born, before he found himself in the stout, gray old city of Kingston in what was then called Upper Canada. It was an extremely hard winter and the St. Lawrence was solidly frozen. So that Starsmeare had no difficulty whatsoever in crossing on the ice to Cape Vincent. That was on the sixteenth day of January. Sleighing in the North Country was good. The English lad had little difficulty in picking up a ride here and a ride there until he was come to Henderson Harbor to the farm of a man named Leffingwell. Here he found employment.

But Starsmeare had not come to America to be a farmer. And so, a year later, when the spring was well advanced, he borrowed a half-dollar from his employer and rode in the stage to Sackett's Harbor. That ancient port was a gay place there at the beginning of the fifties. Its piers were so crowded that vessels lay in the offing, their white sails clearly outlined against the blue of the harbor and the sky, awaiting an opportunity to berth against them. But the vessels had no more than a passing interest for the young Englishman who saw them in all the rush and bustle of the Sackett's Harbor of 1850. For men in the lakeside village were whispering of the coming of the railroad, of the magic presence of the locomotive that so soon was to be visited upon them.

At these rumors the pulse of young Richard Starsmeare quickened. He had seen the railroad already—back home. He had seen it in his home city of London, had seen it cutting in great slits through Camden Town and Somers Town, riding across Lambeth upon seemingly unending brick viaducts. His desire formed itself. He would go to work upon this railroad.... The master of a small coasting ship sailing out from Sackett's Harbor that very afternoon offered him a lift as far as Three Mile Bay. At Three Mile Bay they were to have the railroad. Yet when he arrived there were no signs whatsoever of the iron horse or his special pathway.

"At Chaumont you will find it," they told him there. Off toward Chaumont he trudged. And presently was awarded by the sight of bright yellow stakes set in the fields. He followed these for a little way and found teams and wagons at work. Here was the railroad. The railroad needed men. Specifically it needed young Starsmeare. He found the boss contractor; and went to work for him. He helped get stone out of a nearby quarry for Chaumont bridge. That winter he assisted in the building of Chaumont bridge; a rather pretentious enterprise for those days.

Steadily the Watertown & Rome went ahead. On the Fourth of July, 1851, it was completed to Adams, which was made the occasion of a mighty Independence Day celebration in that brisk village. Upon the arrival of the first train at its depot, a huge parade was formed which marched up into the center of the town, where Levi H. Brown, of Watertown, read the Declaration of Independence, and William Dewey, who had made the building of the Watertown & Rome his life work, delivered a smashing address. Afterwards the procession reformed and returned to the depot where a big dinner was served and the drinking of toasts was in order. There were fireworks in the evening and the Adams Guards honored the occasion with a torchlight parade.

For some weeks the line halted there at Adams. A citizen of Watertown wrote in his diary in August of that year that he had had a fearful time getting home from New York "... The cars only ran to Adams, and I had to have my horse sent down there from Watertown. I had a hard time for a young man...." he complains naïvely.

The railroad was, however, opened to Watertown, its headquarters, its chief town, and the inspiration that had brought it into being, on the evening of September 5, 1851. At eleven o'clock that evening, up to the front of the passenger station, then located near the foot of Stone Street, the first locomotive came into Watertown. I am not at all sure which one of the road's small fleet it was. It had started building operations with four tiny second-hand locomotives which it had garnered chiefly from New England—the Lion, the Roxbury, the Commodore and the Chicopee. Of these the Lion was probably the oldest, certainly the smallest. It had been builded by none other than the redoubtable George Stephenson, himself, in England, some ten or fifteen years before it first came into Northern New York. It was an eight-wheeled engine, of but fourteen tons in weight. So very small was it in fact that it was of very little practical use, that Louis L. Grant, of Rome, who was one of the road's first repair-shop foreman, finally took off the light side-rods between the drivers—the Lion was inside connected, after the inevitable British fashion, and had a V-hook gear and a variable cut-off—and gained an appreciable tractive power for the little engine.

But, at the best, she was hardly a practical locomotive, even for 1851. And soon after the completion of the road to Cape Vincent she was relegated to the round-house there and stored against an emergency. That emergency came three or four years after the opening of the line. A horseman had ridden in great haste to the Cape from Rosiere—then known as LaBranche's Crossing—with news of possible disaster.

"The wood-pile's all afire at the Crossing," he shouted. "Ef the road is a goin' to have any fuel this winter you'd better be hustling down there."

Richard Starsmeare was on duty at the round-house. He hurriedly summoned the renowned Casey Eldredge, then and for many years afterwards a famed engineer of the Rome road and Peter Runk, the extra fireman there. Together they got out the little Lion and made her fast to a flat-car upon which had been put four or five barrels filled with water to extinguish the conflagration. It would have been a serious matter indeed to the road to have had that wood-pile destroyed. It was one of the chief sources of fuel supply of the new railroad. The Lion, with its tiny fire-fighting crew, went post-haste to LaBranche's. But when it had arrived the farmers roundabout already had managed to extinguish the flames.... Casey Eldredge reached for his watch.

"Gee," said he, "we shall have to be getting out of this. The Steamboat Express will be upon our heels. Peter, get the fire up again."

Peter got the fire up. He opened the old fire-box door and thrust an armful of pine into it. The blaze started up with a roar. And then the men who were on the engine found themselves lying on their backs on the grass beside the railroad....

They plowed the Lion out of the fields around LaBranche's for the next two years. Her safety-valve was turned out of the ground by a farmer's boy a good two miles from the railroad. Starsmeare got it and carried it in his tool-box for years thereafter—he quickly rose to the post of engineer and in the days of the Civil War ran a locomotive upon the United States Military Railroad from Washington south through Alexandria to Orange Court House.

So perished the Lion. The little Roxbury's fate was more prosaic. With the flanges upon her driving-wheels ground down and her frame set upon brick piers she became the first powerhouse of the Rome shops. The Commodore and the Chicopee were larger engines. With their names changed they entered the road's permanent engine fleet.

In the meantime the Watertown & Rome was having its own new locomotives built for it in a shop in the United States. Four of the new engines were completed and ready for service about the time that the road was opened into Watertown. The fifth engine, the Orville Hungerford, built like its four immediate predecessors, by William Fairbanks, at Taunton, Mass., was not delivered until the 19th day of that same September, 1851. The Hungerford was quite the best bit of the road's motive-power, then and for a number of years thereafter. She was inside connected—her cylinders and driving-rods being placed inside of the wheels; always the fashion of British locomotives—and it was not until a long time afterwards that she was rebuilt in the Rome shops and the cylinders and rods placed outside, after the present-day American fashion. She was but twenty-one and a half tons in weight all-told, while her four predecessors, the Watertown, the Rome, the Adams and the Kingston, each twenty-two tons and a half.

I have digressed. It still is the evening of the fifth of September, 1851. A great crowd had congregated that evening in the neighborhood of that first, small temporary station at Watertown. The iron horse was greeted with many salvos of applause, the waving of a thousand torches and, it is to be presumed, with the presence of a band. Yet the real celebration over the arrival of the railroad was delayed for nineteen days, when there was a genuine fête. It was first announced by the Reformer on the 4th of September, saying:

"... We are informed by R. B. Doxtater, Esq., the gentlemanly and efficient Superintendent of the Watertown & Rome Railroad, that the public celebration in connection with the opening of this road will take place on Wednesday, the 24th September. This will be a proud day for Jefferson County and we trust that she may wear the honor conferred upon her in a becoming manner. The known liberality of our citizens induces the belief that nothing will be left undone on their part to contribute to the general festivities and interest of the occasion...."

Nothing was left undone. The morning of the 24th of September was ushered in by a salute of guns; thirteen in all, one for each member of the Board of Directors. At 10 o'clock a parade formed in the Public Square, under the direction of General Abner Baker, Grand Marshal of the day, and in the following formation:

Music
Watertown Citizens' Corps

                    Order of The Sons of Temperance
                  Fire Companies of Watertown and Rome
                         Order of Odd Fellows
                       Committee of Arrangements
           Corporate Authorities of Watertown, Kingston, Rome and Utica
                          Clergy and the Press
                Officers, Directors, Engineers and Contractors
                                of the
                        Watertown & Rome Railroad
                         Specially Invited Guests
                 Strangers from Abroad and the Stockholders
                               Citizens

The procession marched down Stone Street to the passenger depot of the new railroad where the special train from Rome arrived at a little after eleven o'clock and was greeted by a salvo of seventy-two guns—one for each mile of completed line. There it reformed, with its accessions from the train and returned to the Public Square where there was unbridled oratory for nearly an hour. After which a return to the depot in which a large collation was served, before the return to the special train for Rome.

So came the railroad to Watertown. By an odd coincidence, the Hudson River Railroad from New York to Albany was finished in almost that same month. It was with a good deal of pride that the resident of Watertown contemplated the fact that he might leave his village by the morning train at five o'clock and be in the metropolis of the New World by six o'clock that same evening. Such speed! Such progress!

In the meantime the Watertown & Rome Railroad had sustained a real loss; in the death, on the morning of Sunday, April 6, 1851, of its first President, the Hon. Orville Hungerford. As the son of one of the earliest pioneers of Watertown, Mr. Hungerford had played no small part in its development. Merchant, banker, Congressman, he had been to it. And to the struggling Watertown & Rome Railroad he was not merely its President, but its financial adviser and friend. It was due to his personal endorsement of the project, as well as that of his bank, that hope in it was finally revived. Then it was that foreign capitalists had their doubts as to its final success dispelled and gave evidence of their faith in the new road by substantial purchases of its securities.

Mr. Hungerford was succeeded as President of the Watertown & Rome by Mr. W. C. Pierrepont, of Brooklyn, who, while in one sense an alien to Jefferson County, was in another and far larger one, not only one of her chief residents but one of her most loyal sons. He, too, had been a powerful friend and advocate of the new road, had worked tirelessly in its behalf. It was his rare opportunity to stand as its President when the locomotive first arrived at Pierrepont Manor, the center of his land holdings, and a very few months later in the same enviable post at Watertown. It was his patient habit to go down to the depot at the Manor evening after evening and with a spy-glass in hand watch the track toward Mannsville for the coming of the evening train. There was no telegraph in those days, of course, and the locomotive's smoke was the only signal of its pending arrival. Neither was there any standard time. Finally it was Pierrepont, himself, who fixed the official time for the road, ascertaining by a skillful use of his chronometer that the suntime at Watertown was just seven minutes and forty-eight seconds slower than that of the City Hall in New York. And so it was officially fixed for the railroad.

Under Mr. Pierrepont's oversight the Watertown & Rome Railroad was finished; through to the village of Chaumont in the fall of 1851, and then in April of the following year to Cape Vincent, its original northern terminal. At this last point elaborate plans were made for a water terminal. Even though the harbor there was not to be protected by a breakwater for many, many years to come, the town was recognized as an international gateway of a very considerable importance. A ferry steamer, The Lady of the Lake, which had attained a distinction from the fact that it was the first upon these northern waters to have staterooms upon its upper decks, was engaged for service between the Cape and the city of Kingston, in Upper Canada. Extensive piers and an elevator were builded there upon the bank of the St. Lawrence, and the large covered passenger station that was so long a familiar landmark of that port.

THE CAPE VINCENT STATION
A Real Landmark of the Old Rome Road, Built in 1852 and Destroyed by a Great Storm in 1895.

For forty years this station stood, even though the span of life of the large hotel that adjoined it was ended a decade earlier by a most devastating fire. But, upon the evening of September 11, 1895, when Conductor W. D. Carnes—best known as "Billy" Carnes—brought his train into the shed to connect with the Kingston boat, a violent storm thrust itself down upon the Cape. In the rainburst that accompanied it, the folk upon the dock sought shelter in the trainshed, and there they were trapped. The wind swept through the open end of that ancient structure and lifted it clear from the ground, dropping it a moment later in a thousand different pieces. It was a real catastrophe. Two persons were killed outright and a number were seriously injured. The event went into the annals of a quiet North Country village, along with the fearful disaster of the steamer Wisconsin, off nearby Grenadier Island, many years before.

With the Cape Vincent terminal completed, the regular operation of trains upon the Watertown & Rome began; formally upon the first day of May, 1852. Six days later the road suffered its first accident, a distressing affair in the neighborhood of Pierrepont Manor. A party of young men in that village had taken upon themselves to "borrow" a hand-car, left by the contractor beside the track and were whirling a group of young women of their acquaintance upon it when around the curve from Adams came a "light" locomotive at high-speed, which crashed into them head-on and killed three of the women almost instantly; and seriously wounded a fourth.

The first employe to lose his life in the service was brakeman George Post, who, on October 13th, of that year, was going forward to lighten the brakes on the northbound freight, as it reached the long down-grade, north of Adams Centre, when he was struck by an overhead bridge and died before aid could reach him.

These men of the North Country were learning that railroading is not all prunes and preserves. They had their own troubles with their new property. For one thing, the engines kept running off the track. There were three locomotive derailments in a single day in 1853 and the Directors asked the Superintendent if he could not be a little more careful in the operation of the line. They also officially chided, quite mildly, one of their number who had contributed twenty-five dollars to the Fourth-of-July celebration in Watertown that summer without asking the consent of the full Board. On the other hand, they quite genially voted annual passes for an indefinite number of years to the widows of Orville Hungerford and of Edmund Kirby as well as their daughters.

It was only two years later than this that there was a change in the Superintendent's office, Job Collamer, who had succeeded its original holder Robert B. Doxtater, being succeeded by Carlos Dutton who was paid the rather astonishing salary, for those days, of $4000 a year. A year later R. E. Hungerford, of Watertown, succeeded Daniel Lee, who was compelled to retire by serious illness as the company's Treasurer and was paid $1500 a year, with an occasional five-hundred-dollar bond from the sinking fund as special compensation at Christmas time. It was about this time also, that John S. Coons, now of Watertown, became station-agent at Brownville, a post which he held for four or five years.

These events were, perhaps, to be reckoned as fairly casual things in the life of a railroad which, to almost any community is life itself. From the beginning the Watertown & Rome played a most important part in the life of the steadily growing territory that it served. Northern New York was finally beginning to come into its own. More than a hundred thousand folk already were residing in Jefferson, St. Lawrence and Lewis counties. No longer was it regarded as a vast wilderness somewhere north of the Erie Canal. Horace Greeley had visited it in the fifties, had lectured in what was afterwards Washington Hall, Watertown, and had been tremendously impressed by Mr. Bradford's portable steam engine. And in 1859 the eyes of the entire land were focused upon Watertown and its immediate surroundings.

That was the year of the big ballooning. John Wise, of Lancaster, Pennsylvania, a well-famed aeronaut, together with three companions—John La Mountain, of Troy, and William Hyde and O. A. Geager, both of Bennington, Vermont—had set forth from St. Louis in the evening in the mammoth balloon, Atlantic, with the expressed intention of sailing to New York City in it. All night long they traveled and sometime before dawn La Mountain fancied that they were over one of the Great Lakes—probably Erie. He awakened his sleeping companions and pointing far over the basket-edge told them that they were passing over the surface of a large body of water.

"You can see the stars below you now," he explained.

And so they were, over Erie. They continued to sail between the stars until dawn, and sometime just before noon they crossed the Niagara River, well in sight of the Falls. Winging their flight at a rate that man had never before made and would not make again for many and many a year to come, the Atlantic traveled the whole length of Ontario before four o'clock in the afternoon and finally made a forced landing not far from the village of Henderson.

The fame that arose from so vast an exploit literally swept around the world. Hyde and Geager had had enough of ballooning and returned to their Vermont home. Wise went back to Lancaster, but La Mountain found an intrepid and a fearless companion in John A. Haddock, at that time editor of the Watertown Reformer, who once had been into the wilds of Labrador and had returned safely from them. Together these men rescued the Atlantic from the tangle of tree-tops into which it had fallen. On August 11th of that same year they announced an ascension from the Fair Grounds in Watertown, accompanied by La Mountain's young cousin, Miss Ellen Moss. And on the twenty-second of the following September the two men made what was destined to be the final ascent of the great Atlantic. The balloon rose high—from the Public Square, this time—and floated off toward the north in a strong wind. In a little less than three hours it traversed some four hundred miles. Then a quick landing was made, in the vast and untrodden Canadian forest, some 150 miles due north of Ottawa, a region even more desolate then than to-day.

For four days the men were lost, hopelessly. Their airship was abandoned in the trees and they made their way afoot as best they might until they came into the path of a party of lumbermen bound for Ottawa. It was another seven days before they had reached the Canadian capital and the outposts of the telegraph—in all eleven endless days before Watertown knew the final result of the foolhardy ascension, and prepared a mighty welcome for them, whom they had given up as dead.

To these really tremendous events in the history of the North Country the Watertown & Rome and the Potsdam & Watertown railroads—of this last, much more in a moment—ran excursions from all Northern New York. Vast throngs of people came upon them. The effect upon the passenger revenues of the two railroads was appreciable upon the occasion of the balloon ascension, just as it had been three summers before, when the first State Fair had been held in Watertown—in a pleasant grove very close to the site of the present Jefferson County Orphans Home. At that time the Rome road had taken in nearly $11,000 in excursion receipts and the Potsdam road, although at that time only completed from Watertown to Gouverneur, more than $5,000. This was used as an argument by the promoters of the second State Fair at Watertown—held on the present county fair grounds in the fall of 1860, for a subscription of a thousand dollars from each of the roads—which was promptly granted.

Yet the Watertown & Rome Railroad needed no excursions for its prosperity. It had prospered greatly; from the beginning. Its four passenger trains a day—two up and two down—were well filled always. Its freight train which ran over the entire length of the line from Rome to Cape Vincent each day did an equally good business. Already it had the third largest freight-car equipment of any railroad in the state. Its success was a tremendous incentive to all other railroad projects in the North Country. From it they all took hope. We have seen long ago the serious efforts that were being made to build a road direct from Sackett's Harbor up the valley of the Black River to Watertown and Carthage and thence across the all-but-impenetrable North Woods to Saratoga. Yet nowhere was it more obvious that a railroad should be builded than between Watertown and some convenient point upon the Northern Railroad, which already was in complete operation between Lake Champlain and Ogdensburgh. Such a railroad presently was builded; taking upon itself the appellation of the Potsdam & Watertown Railroad. And to the consideration of the beginnings of that railroad, a most vital part of the Rome, Watertown & Ogdensburgh, that was as yet unborn, we are now fairly come.

CHAPTER IV
THE POTSDAM & WATERTOWN RAILROAD

A VERY early survey of the Northern Railroad which, as we have already seen, was the pioneer line of the North Country, projected the road between Malone and Ogdensburgh through the prosperous villages of Canton and Potsdam. This survey was rejected. The sponsors of the Northern—almost all of them Boston and New England men and having little personal knowledge of Northern New York and certainly none at all of its possibilities—thrust this preliminary survey away from them. They decided that the road should run between its terminals with as small a deviation from a straight line as possible. So, from Rouse's Point to Ogdensburgh, through Malone, the Northern Railroad ran with long tangents and few curves and both Canton and Potsdam were left aside. Through traffic from the Great Lakes and the St. Lawrence River was all that the early directors of the line could see. Their vision was indeed limited.

Canton and Potsdam began to feel their isolation from these earliest railroad enterprises. They were cut off apparently from railroad communication, either with the East or with the West. The Watertown & Rome Railroad, as planned from Cape Vincent to Rome, would, of course, pass through Watertown, but no one seemed to think of building it east from that village.

So, practically all of St. Lawrence County and the northern end of Jefferson was left without railroad hopes. Dissatisfaction arose, even before the completion of the Watertown & Rome, that so large a territory had been so completely slighted. Potsdam, in particular, felt the indignity that had been heaped upon it. And so it was, that, as far back as 1850, fifty-eight of the public-spirited citizens of that village organized themselves into the Potsdam Railroad Company and proceeded to name as their directors: Joseph H. Sanford, William W. Goulding, Samuel Partridge, Henry L. Knowles, Augustus Fling, Theodore Clark, Charles T. Boswell, Willard M. Hitchcock, William A. Dart, Hiram E. Peck, Aaron T. Hopkins, Charles Cox and Nathan Parmeter. Among the stockholders of this early railroad company were Horace Allen and Liberty Knowles, whose advanced age debarred them from active participation in its work, but who responded liberally to frequent calls for aid in its construction.

Soon after the incorporation of the Potsdam Railroad, it was built, primarily as a branch of some five and one-half miles connecting Potsdam with the Northern Railroad at a point, which, for lack of an immediate better name, was called Potsdam Junction. Afterwards it was renamed Norwood. An attractive village sprang up about the junction, which finally boasted one of the best of the small hotels of the whole North Country; the famed Whitney House, with which the name and fame of the late "Sid" Phelps was so closely connected for so many years.

The success of Potsdam with her railroad and the consequent prosperity that it brought to her stirred the interest and the envy of the neighboring village of Canton; the shire-town of St. Lawrence. Gouverneur spruced up also. The St. Lawrence towns began to coöperate. To them came a great community of interest from the northerly townships and villages of Jefferson as well—Antwerp, Philadelphia and Evan's Mills in particular. The demand for a railroad between Watertown and Potsdam began to take a definite form.

It was not an easy task to which the towns and men of St. Lawrence and of Jefferson had set themselves. Its financial aspects were portentous, to put it mildly. The money for the Northern Railroad had come from New England. That for the Watertown & Rome also had come with a comparative ease. Watertown even then was a rich and promising industrial center and there seemed to be genuine financial opportunities for a railroad that would connect it with the outer world. But St. Lawrence County, there at the beginning of the fifties, was poor and undeveloped. Necessarily, the money for its railroad would have to come from its own territory. Nevertheless, undaunted by difficulties, these men of that territory set about to build a railroad from Potsdam to Watertown. They dared much. Theirs was the spirit of the true pioneer, the same spirit that was building a college at Canton and had built academies at Gouverneur and at Potsdam, and that was planning in every way for the future development of the North Country.

These men knew more than a little of the resources of their townships. They whispered among themselves of the wealth of their minerals. Along the county-line between St. Lawrence and Jefferson, in the neighborhood of Keene's Station, there stand to-day unused iron mines of a considerable magnitude. Flooded and for the moment deserted, these mines house some of the greatest of the untouched treasures of Northern New York; vast deposits of red hematite, exceeding in percentage value even the famous fields of the Mesaba district of Lake Superior. In the course of this narrative I shall refer again to these Keene mines. For the moment consider them as a monument—a somewhat neglected monument to be sure—to the vision and persistence of James Sterling.

It was largely due to the enterprise of this pioneer of Jefferson County that mines and blast furnaces sprang up, not only at Keene's but at Sterlingville and Lewisburgh as well. He built many of the highways and bridges both of Antwerp and of Rossie. Yet, in the closing days of the fifties, he was doomed to bitter disappointments. The great panic of 1857 and the inrush of cheap iron that followed in its wake were quite too much for him, and the man who had been known through the entire state as the "Iron King of Northern New York" died in 1863, from a general physical and mental breakdown, due in no small part to the collapse of his fortunes.

I anticipate, we were talking of railroads, not of men. Yet, somehow, men must forever weave themselves into the web of a narrative such as this. And no fair understanding can ever be had of the difficulties under which the railroads of the North Country were born without an understanding of the difficulties under which the men who helped give them birth labored. To return once again to the main thread of our story, the agitation for the building of a railroad between Watertown and Potsdam followed closely upon the heels of the completion of the Northern Railroad and the branch Potsdam Railroad, from it to the fine village of that name. Stock in the Northern Railroad had been sold both there and in Canton, even though the road when completed had passed each by. The men who held that stock wanted to come to the aid of the newer project. With their money tied up in the elder of the two, they were quite helpless. Eventually their release was brought about, and the money that came to them from the sale of their securities of the Northern was reinvested in those of the Potsdam & Watertown Railroad, just coming into being.

A meeting was held in Watertown in July, 1851 (the year of the completion of the Watertown & Rome Railroad) and E. N. Brodhead employed to make a preliminary survey of the proposed line; which would be followed immediately with maps and estimates. He went to his task without delay, and rendered a full report on the possibilities of the road at a meeting held at Gouverneur on January 9, 1852. There were no dissenting voices in regard to the proposed line. So it was, that then and there, the Potsdam & Watertown Railroad was organized permanently, with the following directors:

Edwin Dodge, Gouverneur	W. E. Sterling, Gouverneur
Zenas Clark, Potsdam	Joseph H. Sanford, Potsdam
Samuel Partridge, Potsdam	William W. Goulding, Potsdam
E. Miner, Canton	Barzillai Hodskin, Canton

A. M. Adsit, Colton   H. B. Keene, Antwerp

O. V. Brainard, Watertown   Howell Cooper, Watertown

Hiram Holcomb, Watertown

The old minute-book of the Directors of this early railroad has been carefully preserved in the village of Potsdam. It is a narrative of a really stupendous effort, of struggles against adversity, of undaunted courage, of optimism and of faith. It relates unemotionally what the Directors did, but between the lines one also reads of the grave situations that confronted them; not once, but again and again. And there lies the real drama of the founding of the Potsdam & Watertown.

The first meeting of the Directors was held, as we have just seen, on January 9, 1852. Most of the men, who were that day elected as Directors, had gone on that day to Gouverneur—many others too. Watertown, Gouverneur, Canton and Potsdam were present in their citizens, men of worth and distinction in their home communities. Their families are yet represented in Northern New York, and succeeding generations owe to them a debt of gratitude for their unselfish work in that early day. For what could there be of selfishness in a task which promised so much of worry and responsibility, and so little of any immediate financial return?

It was planned, that January day in Gouverneur, that work should be begun at both ends of the line and carried forward simultaneously, until the construction crews should meet; somewhere between Potsdam and Watertown. At an adjourned meeting, held ten days later at the American Hotel in Watertown, it was formally resolved that; "all persons who have subscribed toward the expenses of the survey of the Potsdam & Watertown Railroad Company ... shall be entitled to a credit on the stock account for the amount so subscribed and paid." At the same meeting it was decided that a committee consisting of Messrs. Farwell, Holcomb and Dodge be appointed to confer with the officers of the Watertown & Rome in regard to the construction of a branch into the village of Watertown. It will be remembered that in that early day the railroad did not approach the village nearer than what is now known as the junction, at the foot of Stone Street.

Progress was beginning, in real earnest. A third meeting was held on February 26—again at Gouverneur, at Van Buren's Hotel—and the following officers chosen:

President, EDWIN DODGE, Gouverneur

Vice-President, ZENAS CLARK, Potsdam
Secretary, HENRY L. KNOWLES, Potsdam
Treasurer, DANIEL LEE, Watertown

Mr. Lee was also Treasurer of the Watertown & Rome. His Potsdam & Watertown compensation was fixed a little later at $600 annually. Four years later he was succeeded as Treasurer by William W. Goulding, of Potsdam, who was engaged at a salary of a thousand dollars a year.

At that same Gouverneur meeting a memorial was prepared for the Trustees of the Village of Watertown. It asked, as an important link of the pathway for the new railroad, the use of Factory Street for its entire length. Factory Street, as we have already seen, was one of the most aristocratic, as well as one of the prettiest streets of the town. So great was Watertown's appreciation of the advantages that were to accrue to it by the completion of the line steel highway to the north that the permission was finally granted by the Trustees, not, however, without a considerable opposition.

So was our Potsdam & Watertown fairly started upon its important career. A fund of something over $750,000 having been raised for its construction, offices were opened at 6 Washington Street, Watertown, and definite preparations made toward the actual building of the road. The breaking of ground was bound to be preceded by a stout financial campaign. Money was tight. And remember all the while, if you will, the real paucity of it in the North Country of those days. And yet early in 1853, it was found necessary to increase the capital stock to $2,000,000, in itself, an act requiring some courage; yet after all, it might have required more courage not to take the step. For, of a truth, the company needed the money.

Gradually committees were appointed, not only to look after this and other vexing financial questions, but also to supervise the location of the line as well as to provide suitable station grounds and buildings. There were many meetings of the Board before the road was definitely located; there must have been much bitterness of spirit and of discussion. Hermon wanted the road, and so an alternative route between Canton and Gouverneur was surveyed to include it. In 1853 the Chief Engineer was directed "to cause the middle route (so designated in Mr. Brodhead's report) in the towns of Canton and DeKalb to be sufficiently surveyed for location as soon as practicable, unless upon examination, the Engineer shall believe the railroad can be constructed upon the Hermon route, so called, as cheaply and with as much advantage to the company, and that in such case he cause that route to be surveyed, instead of the middle route." But stock subscriptions were light in Hermon and engineering difficult on its route, and finally the "middle" and present route by the way of DeKalb and Richville was selected. Similarly local discouragements turned the line sharply toward the North, after crossing the Racket River at Potsdam, instead of toward the South, and, a more direct route originally surveyed, toward Canton.

The location of the station grounds was another source of fruitful discussion. In this regard, Gouverneur seems to have given the greatest concern. Many committees wrestled with the problem of its depot site. In the old minute-book, rival locations appear and, upon one occasion, the matter having simmered down to a choice between the present station grounds and prospective ones on the other side of the river, the Chief Engineer was directed to survey out both locations and set stakes, so that the whole Board could visit the village and see the thing for itself.

By 1854 distinct progress had been made. At a meeting held on February 4th of that year, Messrs. Cooper, Brainard and Holcomb, of the Directorate, were authorized as a committee to enter into negotiations for the purchase of iron rails for the road, and to complete the purchase of 2500 tons of these, by sale of the bonds of the company, "or otherwise." The financial end of the transaction was apt always to be the most difficult part of it. Yet somehow these were almost always solved. The Watertown & Rome road guaranteed some of the bonds of the Potsdam & Watertown and Erastus Corning, of Albany, and John H. Wolfe, of New York, loaned it considerable sums of money. Construction proceeded, and on May 4, 1854, the Directors decided to send 650 tons of the new iron to the easterly terminus of the road; the remainder to the westerly building forces.

In the fall of that year, a considerable amount of track having been laid down, the Directors looked toward the purchase of rolling stock. At their November meeting they decided to buy the engine Montreal, and its tender, from the Watertown & Rome, at a cost of $4,500; also two baggage and "post-office" cars, at $750 each. Which provided for the beginning of operation at the west end of the road.

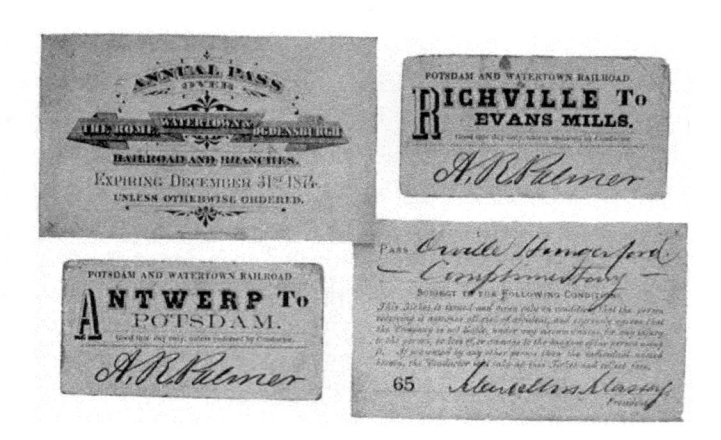

EARLY RAILROAD TICKETS
Including an Annual Pass Issued by President Marcellus Massey, of the R. W. & O.

But the east end needed rolling-stock as well—a considerable gap still intervened between the rail-heads of each incomplete section. So toward the East, the Directors of the Potsdam & Watertown turned their attention. They found some rolling stock in the hands of a man in Plattsburgh; "Vilas, of Plattsburgh" is his sole designation in their minutes. This Vilas, it would appear, was a hard-headed Clinton County business man who seemed to have but little confidence in the financial soundness of the Potsdam & Watertown. Nothing of the gambler appears in Vilas. He did not believe in taking chances. He had a locomotive and two cars that he would sell—for cash. Eventually, he sold them—for cash. Some of the Directors of the P. & W. bought them, themselves, paying out their own hard-earned cash for them; and recouping themselves by accepting pay in installments from the company.

Yet the possible danger in a continuance of such practices was recognized even in that early day, and in order to avoid similar situations arising at some later time, I find in the old tome a resolution reading: "Whereas in raising money and carrying on the operations of our company for the completion of the road, the unanimous coöperation of its Directors is necessary, particularly in matters involving personal pecuniary liability, therefore: Resolved; That each Director now present pledge himself to endorse and guaranty all notes and bills of exchange required by the committee on finance to be used in accordance with the preceding resolution ... and that we hold it to be the duty of all Directors of this company to do the same."

From time to time a note of pathos creeps into these old minutes and one catches a glimpse of the trials and struggles of the little company. For instance: "Resolved: That in our struggles for the construction of the road of this company, we have not failed to appreciate the liberal spirit with which we have been met and the encouragement and aid often freely afforded us by Hon. George V. Hoyle, Superintendent of the Northern Railroad, and we avail ourselves of this occasion to express to him, individually and as Superintendent, and through him to those associated with him the management of that road, our sense of obligation, indulging the hope that we shall yet be able in the same spirit to reciprocate all his kindness, and that the interest of Mr. Hoyle and his road may be abundantly promoted by our success."

And then, finally, success! In the faded minutes Secretary Knowles triumphantly records that "On the morning of the fifth of February, 1857, a passenger train left Watertown at about nine o'clock a. m., with many of the officers of the company and invited friends, passed leisurely over the entire road to its junction with the Northern Railroad, thence with the Superintendent of that road to Ogdensburgh, arriving at Ogdensburgh at about four o'clock and returned the next day to Watertown."

This is not to be interpreted, however, as meaning that the Potsdam & Watertown was immediately ready for business. There remained much work to be done in completing the track and the roadbed, station buildings, equipment, and the other appurtenances necessary for a going railroad. The contractors, Phelps, Mattoon and Barnes, who also had built the Watertown & Rome, had unpaid balances still remaining. There had been numerous and one or two rather serious disagreements between the company and its contractors. Finally these were all settled by a final cash payment of $100,000, in addition, of course, to what had been paid before. In order to make this large payment—for that day, at least—it became necessary to bond the property still again; this time by a second mortgage—which was made around $200,000, so that the road might be made completely ready for business.

Details which indicate the rapidly approaching time of such completion soon begin to appear in the minutes. A committee is appointed to procure a Superintendent—George B. Phelps, of Watertown, was appointed to this post. Freight agents are directed to turn over their receipts to the Treasurer weekly, ticket agents daily. The Board took its business seriously and several meetings about this time were called for seven, half past seven and eight o'clock in the morning, although, of course, this might mean that the railroad business was gotten out of the way early, leaving the day free for regular occupations. The vexed question of the station grounds at Gouverneur was settled definitely early in 1857, and the executive committee was instructed to erect on the "station grounds at Gouverneur a building similar to the one at Antwerp in the speediest and most economical manner." To this day the Antwerp building survives, but Gouverneur, like Potsdam, for more than a decade past has rejoiced in the possession of a new and ornate passenger station.

It was not until June, 1857, that a definite passenger service was established upon the line from Watertown, where it connected with the trains of the W. & R., and thus to the present village of Norwood, seventy-five miles distant. It is worth noting here that a few years after this was accomplished a branch line was constructed from a point two miles distant from the old village of DeKalb, and destined to be known to future fame as DeKalb Junction, straight through to Ogdensburgh, but eighteen miles distant. DeKalb Junction also had a famous hotel which for many years "fed" the trains and "fed" them well. In its earlier days this tavern was known as the Goulding House; in more recent years, however, it has been the Hurley House, so named from the late Daniel Hurley, one of the most popular and successful hotelmen in all the North Country.

The passenger trains of the Potsdam road were operated out of the new station in Watertown, just back of the Woodruff House—which we shall see in another chapter. For a time there was no train service for travelers between its station and that of the Rome road at the foot of Stone Street, the transfer between them being made by stages. But soon this was rectified and the one o'clock train, north from Watertown, allowed considerably more than an hour for connection after the arrival of the train from Rome, which gave abundant time for the consumption of one of Proprietor Dorsey's fine meals at the Woodruff. It was a good meal and not high-priced. The charge per day for three of them and a night's lodging thrown in was fixed at but $1.50.

The early train which left Watertown at sharp six o'clock in the morning—afterwards it was fixed at a slightly later hour—made connection at Potsdam Junction with the through train on the Northern for Rouse's Point and, going by that roundabout way, a traveler might hope to reach Montreal in the evening of the day that he had left Watertown—if he enjoyed good fortune. Whilst upon the completion of the short line a few years later between DeKalb Junction and Ogdensburgh, one could reach the Canadian metropolis in an even more direct fashion, by the ferry steamer Transit to Prescott, and then over the Grand Trunk Railway, just coming into the heyday of its fame. Watertown no longer was cut off from rail communication with the North.

The Potsdam & Watertown though now fairly launched, operating trains, and, from all external evidences at least, doing a fair business, nevertheless was grievously burdened with its grave financial difficulties. On May 16, 1857, a special finance committee, consisting of Messrs. Phelps, Cooper and Goulding, was appointed with power to carry along the company's growing floating debt, and in October of that selfsame year the President joined with them in their appeals to the creditors to have a little more patience. In the following spring the Directors discussed the propriety of asking the Legislature for an act exempting from taxation all railroads in the state that were not paying their dividends.

The Potsdam road certainly was not paying its dividends. Not only this, but, on May 26, 1859, interest on the second mortgage, being unpaid for six months, the trustees under the mortgage took possession of the property and the Directors in meeting approved of the action. Such a step quite naturally agitated the first mortgage holders, who began to protest. In August, 1859, the P. & W. Board disclaimed any purpose whatsoever to repudiate the payment of principal or interest upon its first mortgage bonds, or its contingent obligation to the Watertown & Rome Railroad. It invited the Directors of that larger and more prosperous road to attend a joint meeting wherein the earnings of the Potsdam & Watertown might be applied to the payment of the coupons upon its first mortgage bonds. There was a growing community of interest between the two roads, anyway. The one was the natural complement to the other. Such a community of interest led, quite naturally, to a merger of the properties. In June, 1860, it was announced that the Watertown & Rome had gained financial control of the Potsdam & Watertown. Soon after the Rome, Watertown & Ogdensburgh was officially born and a new chapter in the development of Northern New York was begun.

CHAPTER V
THE FORMATION OF THE R. W. & O.

THAT the Watertown & Rome and the Potsdam & Watertown Railroads would have merged in any event was, from the first, almost a foregone conclusion. Their interests were too common to escape such inevitable consolidation. The actual union of the two properties was accomplished in the very early sixties (July 4, 1861) and for the merged properties—the new trunk-line of the North Country, if you please—the rather euphonious and embracing title of the Rome, Watertown & Ogdensburgh Railroad was chosen. It was at that time that the branch was built from DeKalb to Ogdensburgh. A combined directorate was chosen from the governing bodies of the two merged roads—I shall not take the trouble to set it down here and now—and Mr. Pierrepont was chosen as the President of the new property, with Marcellus Massey, of Brooklyn, as its Vice-President, R. E. Hungerford as Secretary and Treasurer, H. T. Frary as General Ticket Agent, C. C. Case as General Freight Agent and Addison Day as General Superintendent. Whilst the general offices of the company were in Watertown, its shops and general operating offices, at that time, were in Rome. It was in this latter city that Addison Day was first located. Day was a resident of Rochester. He refused to remove his home from that city, but spent each week-end with his family there.

He was a conspicuous figure upon the property, coming as the successor to a number of superintendents, each of whom had served a comparatively short time in office—Robert B. Doxtater, Job Collamer and Carlos Dutton, were Addison Day's predecessors as Superintendents upon the property. These men had been local in their opportunity. To Day was given a real job; that of successfully operating 189 miles of a pretty well-built and essential railroad. Yet his annual salary was fixed at but $2500, as compared with the $4000 paid to Dutton. Later however Day was raised to $3000 a year.

The main shops of the company, as I have just said, were then situated in Rome. They were well equipped for that day and employed about one hundred men, under William H. Griggs, the road's first Master Mechanic. A smaller shop, of approximately one-half the capacity and used chiefly for engine repairs and freight-car construction, was located at Watertown, just back of the old engine house on Coffeen Street.

WATERTOWN IN 1865
Showing the First Passenger Station of the Potsdam & Watertown.
Taken from the Woodruff House Tower.

But Watertown's chief comfort was in its passenger station, which stood in the rear of the well-famed Woodruff House. Norris M. Woodruff had completed his hotel at about the same time that the railroad first reached Watertown. It was a huge structure—reputed to be at that time the largest hotel in the United States west of New York City; and even the far-famed Astor House of that metropolis, had no dining-salon which in height and beauty quite equalled the dining-room of the Woodruff House. Mr. Woodruff had given the railroad the site for its passenger station in the rear of his hotel, on condition that the chief passenger terminal of the company should forever be maintained there, which has been done ever since. Yet the chief passenger station of the R. W. & O. of 1861 was a simple affair indeed. Builded in brick it afterwards became the wing of the larger station that was torn down to be replaced by the present station a decade ago. It was not until 1870 that the three story "addition" to the original station was built and the first station restaurant at Watertown opened, in charge of Col. A. T. Dunton, from Bellows Falls, Vt. After the fashion of the time, its opening was signalized by a banquet.

In front of me there lies a very early time-table of the Rome, Watertown & Ogdensburgh Railroad. It bears the date, April 20, 1863, and apparently is the twelfth to be issued in the history of the road. It is signed by Addison Day, as Superintendent.

On this sheet, the chief northbound train, No. 7, Express and Mail, left Rome at four o'clock each afternoon, reaching Watertown at 7:05 p. m., and leaving there twenty minutes later, arrived at Ogdensburgh at 10:30 p. m. The return movement of this train, was as No. 2, leaving Ogdensburgh at 4:25 o'clock in the morning, passing Watertown at 7:10 o'clock and reaching Rome at 10:35 a. m. In addition to this double movement each day, there was a similar one of accommodation trains; No. 1, leaving Rome at 2:35 o'clock each morning, arriving and leaving Watertown at 6:20 and 6:40 a. m., respectively, and reaching Ogdensburgh at 10:10 a. m. As No. 8, the accommodation returned, leaving Ogdensburgh at 4:30 p. m., passing Watertown at 8:20 p. m., and arriving at Rome at 12:20 a. m. Apparently folk who traveled in those days cared little about inconvenient hours of arrival or departure.

There were connecting trains upon both the Cape Vincent and the Potsdam Junction branches—the branch from Richland to Oswego was just under construction—and a scheduled freight train over the entire line each day. Yet there, still, was an almost entire absence of mid-day passenger service.

Gradually this condition of things must have improved; for in Hamilton Child's Jefferson County Gazetteer and Business Directory, for 1866, I find the Rome, Watertown & Ogdensburgh advertising three fast passenger trains a day in each direction over the entire main line, in addition to connections, not only for Cape Vincent and for Potsdam Junction, but also over the new branch from Richland through Pulaski to Oswego. Pulaski, humiliated in the beginning by the refusal of the Watertown & Rome to lay its rails within four miles of that county-seat village, finally had received the direct rail connection, that she had so long coveted.

In that same advertisement there first appears announcement of through sleeping-cars, between Watertown and New York, an arrangement which continued for a number of years thereafter, then was abandoned for many years, but, under the bitter protests of the citizens of Watertown and other Northern New York communities, was finally restored in 1891 as an all-the-year service.

Upon the ancient time table of 1863 there appear the names of the old stations, the most of which have come down unchanged until to-day. One of them has disappeared both in name and existence, Centreville, two miles south of Richland, while the adjacent station of Albion long since became Altmar. Potsdam Junction we have already seen as Norwood, while nice dignified old Sanford's Corners long since suffered the unspeakable insult of being renamed, by some latter-day railroad official, Calcium. A similar indignity at that time was heaped upon Adams Centre, being known officially for a time as Edison!

The Centre rebelled. It had no quarrel with Mr. Edison. On the contrary, it held the highest esteem for that distinguished inventor. But for the life of it, it could not see why the name of a nice old-fashioned Seventh-Day-Baptist town should be sacrificed for the mere convenience of a telegrapher's code. It was quite bad enough when Union Square, over on the Syracuse line, was forced, willy-nilly, to become Maple View, and Holmesville, Fernwood. Neither were the marvels of the lexicographers of the Postoffice Department, under which all manner of strange changes were made in the spelling of old North Country names (think of Sackett's Harbor, time-honored government military and naval station, reduced to a miserable "Sacket!") germane to Adams Centre's problem. Adams Centre it was christened in the beginning, and Adams Centre it proposed to remain. And after a brief but brisk fight with railroad and postoffice officials, it succeeded in regaining its birthright.

Early in June, 1872, William C. Pierrepont retired as President of the Rome, Watertown & Ogdensburgh and was succeeded by Marcellus Massey, the third holder of that important post of honor in the North Country. Mr. Massey, although for the greater part of his life also a resident of Brooklyn, was of Jefferson County stock, a brother of Hart and of Solon Massey. He gave his whole time and interest to the steady upbuilding of the road. Gradually it was coming to a point where it was considered, without exception, the best operated railroad in the State of New York, if not in the entire land. Sometimes it was called the Nickel Plate, although that name nowadays is generally reserved for the brisk trunk line—officially the New York, Chicago & St. Louis—that operates from Buffalo, through Cleveland to Chicago.

The R. W. & O. was in fact at that time an extremely high-grade railroad property; it was the pride of Watertown, of the entire North Country as well. Mr. Massey used to say that as a dividend payer—its annual ten per cent came as steadily as clock-striking—his road could not be beat; particularly in a day when many railroad investments were regarded as very shaky things indeed. The crash of the Oswego Midland, which was to come a few years later, was to add nothing to the confidence of investors in this form of investment.

Steadily Mr. Massey and his co-workers sought to perfect the property. The service was a very especial consideration in their minds. A moment ago we saw the time table of 1863 in brief, now consider how it had steadily been improved, in the course of another eight years.

In 1871 the passenger service of the R. W. & O. consisted of two trains through from Rome to Ogdensburgh without change. The first left Rome at 4:30 a. m., passed through Watertown at 7:38 a. m., and arrived at Ogdensburgh at 11:15 a. m. The second left Rome at 1:00 p. m., passed through Watertown at 4:17 p. m., and arrived at Ogdensburgh at 7:10 p. m. Returning the first of these trains left Ogdensburgh at 6:08 a. m., passed through Watertown at 9:20 a. m., and arrived at Rome at 12:10 p. m.: the second left Ogdensburgh at 3:00 p. m., passed through Watertown at 6:35 p. m., and reached Rome and the New York Central at 9:05 p. m. The similarity between these trains and those upon the present time-card, the long established Seven and One and Four and Eight, is astonishing. Put an important train but once upon a time card, and seemingly it is hard to get it off again.

In addition to these four important through trains there were others: The Watertown Express, leaving Rome at 5:30 p. m. and "dying" at Watertown at 9:05 p. m., was the precursor of the present Number Three. The return movement of this train was as the New York Express, leaving Watertown at 8:10 a. m. and reaching Rome at 11:35 a. m. There were also three trains a day in each direction on the Cape Vincent, and Oswego branches and two on the one between DeKalb and Potsdam Junctions.

For a railroad to render real service it must have, not alone good track—in those early days the Rome road, as it was known colloquially, gave great and constant attention to its right of way—but good engines. Up to about 1870 these were exclusively wood-burners, many of them weighing not more than from twenty to twenty-five tons each. They were of a fairly wide variety of type. While the output of the Rome Locomotive Works was always favored, there were numbers of engines from the Rhode Island, the Taunton and the Schenectady Works.

Thirty-eight of these wood-burning engines formed the motive-power equipment of the Rome road in the spring of 1869. Their names—locomotives in those days invariably were named—were as follows:

1. Watertown
2. Rome
3. Adams
4. Kingston
5. O. Hungerford

20. Potsdam
21. Ontario
22. Montreal
23. New York
24. Ogdensburgh

6. Col. Edwin Kirby
7. Norris Woodruff
8. Camden
9. J. L. Grant
10. Job Collamer
11. Jefferson
12. R. B. Doxtater
13. O. V. Brainard
14. North Star
15. T. H. Camp
16. Silas Wright
17. Antwerp
18. Wm. C. Pierrepont
19. St. Lawrence
25. Oswego
26. D. DeWitt
27. D. Utley
28. M. Massey
29. H. Moore
30. C. Comstock
31. S. F. Phelps
32. Col. Wm. Lord
33. H. Alexander, Jr.
34. Roxbury
35. Com. Perry
36. C. E. Bill
37. Gen. S. D. Hungerford
38. Gardner Colby

Of this considerable fleet the Antwerp was perhaps the best known. Oddly enough she was the engine that the directors of the Potsdam & Watertown had purchased from "Vilas, of Plattsburgh." She was then called the Plattsburgh, but upon her coming to the R. W. & O. she was already renamed Antwerp. Inside connected, like the O. Hungerford, she also was a product of the old Taunton works down in Eastern Massachusetts. Her bright red driving wheels made her a conspicuous figure on the line.

The Camden was also an inside connected engine. The Ontario and the Potsdam and the Montreal were other acquisitions from the Potsdam & Watertown. The Potsdam had a picture of a lion painted upon her front boiler door, the work of some gifted local artist, unknown to present fame. She came to the North Country as the Chicopee from the Springfield Locomotive Works, and with her came, as engineer and fireman, respectively, the famous Haynes brothers, Orville and Rhett. Henry Batchelder, a brother of the renowned Ben, who comes later into this narrative, and who is now a resident of Potsdam, well recalls the first train that made the trip between that village and Canton. Made up of flat-cars with temporary plank seats atop of them, and hauled by the Potsdam, it brought excursionists into Canton to enjoy the St. Lawrence County Fair. That was in the year of 1855, and the railroad was only completed to a point some two miles east of Canton. From that point the travelers walked into town.

Mr. Batchelder also remembers that the engineers and firemen of that early day invariably wore white shirts upon their locomotives. The old wood-burners were never so hard as the coal-burners on the apparel of their crews. They were wonderful little engines and, as we shall see in a moment, had a remarkable ability for speed with their trains. The Antwerp in particular had rare speed. Those red drivers of hers were the largest upon the line. And when Jeff Wells was at her throttle and those red heels of hers were digging into the iron, men reached for their watches.

No true history of the Rome, Watertown & Ogdensburgh might ever be written without mention of Jefferson B. Wells. In truth he was the commodore of the old locomotive fleet. For skill and daring and precision in the handling of an engine he was never excelled. Although bearing a certain uncanny reputation for being in accidents, he was blamed for none of them. Whether at the lever of his two favorites, the T. H. Camp and the Antwerp, or in later years as captain of the "44" he was in his element in the engine-cab. The "44" spent most of the later years of her life, and of Wells', in service upon the Cape Vincent branch. I can remember it standing at Watertown Junction, sending an occasional soft ring of grayish smoke off into the blue skies above. And distinctly can I recall Jeff Wells himself, a large-eyed, tallish man, fond of a good joke, or a good story, a man with a keen zest in life itself. He was a good poker player. It is related of him, that one night, while engaged in a pleasant game at Cape Vincent, word came from Watertown ordering him to his engine for a special run down to the county-seat and back.

For a moment old Jeff hesitated. He liked poker. But then the trained soul of the railroader triumphed. He threw his hand down upon the table—it was a good hand, too—and turning toward the call-boy said:

"Son, I'll be at the round house within ten minutes."

That was Wells; best at home in the engine-cab, and, I think no engine-cab was ever quite the same to him as that of the speedy Antwerp, with John Leasure on the fireman's side of the cab—Leasure was pretty sure to have previously bedecked the Antwerp with a vast variety of cedar boughs, flags and the like—and the President's car on behind. This, in later years, was sure to be the old parlor-car, Watertown, gayly furbished for the occasion. This special was sure to be given the right-of-way over all other trains on the line that day; all the switch-points being ordered spiked, in order to avoid the possibility of accidents. Yet, on at least one occasion—at DeKalb Junction—this practice nearly led to a serious mishap. Mr. Massey's train had swept past the little depot there and around the curve onto the Ogdensburgh branch at seventy miles an hour. For once there had been a miscalculation. The little train veered terribly as it struck the branch-line rails; the directors were thrown from their comfortable seats in the parlor-car, and poor Billy Lanfear, of Cape Vincent, the fireman, was nearly carromed from his place in the cab. At the last fractional part of a second he succeeded in catching hold of the engineer's window as he started to shoot out.

The wood-burners were not supposed to be fast engines—a great many of them in the early days of the R. W. & O. had small drivers and this was an added handicap to their speed. But sixty miles an hour was not out of the question for them. Mr. Richard Holden, of Watertown, who started his railroad career in the eating-house of the old station in that city, still recalls several trips that he made in the cab of the engines on the Cape branch. It had a fairly close schedule at the best, connecting at Watertown Junction with Number Three up from Rome in the afternoon, and turning and coming back in time to make connections with Number Six down the line. It frequently would happen that Three would be fifteen or twenty minutes late, which would mean a good deal of hustling on the part of the Cape train to make her fifty mile run and turn-around and still avoid delaying Number Six. But both Casey Eldredge and Chris Delaney, the engineers on the branch at that time, could do it: Jeff Wells was still on the main line and unwilling then to accept the easier Cape branch run, which afterwards he was very glad to take.

"The air-brake was unknown at that time," says Mr. Holden, "all trains being stopped by the brakeman, assisted by the fireman, a brake being upon the tender of all the engines. When some of these fast trains were running, I used to take a great delight in riding on the engine, and remember the running-time of the trip was thirty-five minutes, which included stops at Brownville, Limerick, Chaumont and Three Mile Bay, my recollection being that the station at Rosiere was not open at that time. Deducting the time used for stops the actual running time would average sixty miles an hour. All engines used on passenger trains had small driving-wheels and it will be remembered that all passenger trains, except One and Six, consisted of but a baggage-car and two coaches, consequently an engine could get a train under good headway much faster than engines with the heavy equipment in use at the present time."

In all these statements in regard to the speed of the trains upon the early R. W. & O. it should not be forgotten that for the first twelve or thirteen years of the road's existence, it had to worry along without telegraphic or any other form of rapid interstation communication. It was not until 1863 or 1864 that its trains were despatched upon telegraphic orders; and even these were of the crudest possible form. The "Nineteen" had not yet been evolved. A slip of paper torn from the handiest writing block and scribbled in fairly indecipherable hieroglyphics was the train order of those beginnings of modern railroading. The telegraph order, instead of being a real help to the locomotive engineer, was apt to be one of the puzzles and the banes of his existence.

It was in 1866 that a railroad telegraph office was first established at Watertown Junction and D. N. Bosworth engaged as despatcher there. According to the recollections of Mr. W. D. Hanchette, of that city, who is the nestor of all things telegraphic in Northern New York, Bosworth was soon followed by a Mr. Warner, who was not, himself, a telegraphic operator, but who had to be assisted by one. A Canadian, named Monk, was one of the first of these. Warner was finally succeeded as despatcher at Watertown Junction by N. B. Hine, a brother of Omar A. Hine and of A. C. Hine—all of them much identified with the history of the Rome road. N. B. Hine remained with the road for a long season of years as its train despatcher, eventually moving his office from the Junction to the enlarged passenger station back of the Woodruff House in Watertown.

He learned his trade in the summer before Fort Sumter was fired upon; using a small, home-made, wooden key at his father's farm, somewhere back of DeKalb. A year after he had obtained his railroad job, Omar Hine was appointed operator at Richland, opening the first telegraph office at that place, and becoming its station agent as well. From Richland he was promoted to the more important, similar post at Norwood. When he left Norwood, Mr. Hine became a conductor upon the main line. In that service he remained until the comparatively recent year of 1887.

About the time that he was assigned to Richland, his brother, A. C. Hine, was appointed operator and helper at the neighboring station of Sandy Creek. So from a single North Country farm sprang three expert telegraphers and railroaders. When they began their career, but a single wire stretched all the way from Watertown to Ogdensburgh; and the movement of trains by telegraph was occasional, not regular nor standardized. A second wire was strung the entire length of the line in the fall of 1866 and in the following spring, Mr. Bosworth began the difficult task of trying to work a systematic method of telegraphic despatching, and gradually brought the engineers of the road into a real coöperation with his plan, a thing much more difficult to accomplish than might be at first imagined.

Those old-time engineers of the road were good men; but some of them were a trifle "sot" in their ways. Their habits were not things easily changed.

The full list of these old-time engineers of the R. W. & O. would run to a considerable length. Remember again Orve Haynes—something of an engine-runner was he—who afterwards went down to St. Louis to become Master Mechanic upon the Iron Mountain road. The J. L. Grant was named after a Master Mechanic of the R. W. & O., who eventually became an assistant superintendent. The Grant was in steady use upon the Cape branch prior to the coming of the "44." A good engineer in those days was a good mechanic—invariably. Repair facilities were few and far between. The ingenuity and quick wit of the man in the engine-cab more than once was called into play. Engine failures were no less frequent then than now.

Ben. F. Batchelder first came to fame as a well-known engineer of that early decade; John Skinner was another. There was D. L. Van Allen and Louis Bouran and John Mortimer and Casey Eldredge and Asa Rowell and old "Parse" Hines, and George Schell and Jim Cheney—that list does indeed run to lengths. In a later generation came Nathaniel R. Peterson ("Than") and Conrad Shaler and Frank W. Smith and George H. Hazleton, and Frank Taylor, and Charles Vogel—but again I must desist. This is a history, not a necrology. It is hardly fair to pick but a few names, out of so many deserving ones.

The most of the engineers of that day have gone. A very few remain. One of these is Frank W. Smith, of Watertown, who to-day (1922) has retired from his engine-cab, but remains one of the expert billiard players in the Lincoln League of that city.

Mr. Smith entered upon his railroad career on November 9, 1866, at the rather tender age of seventeen, as a wiper in the old round house in Coffeen Street, Watertown. In those days all the engines upon the line still were wood-burners. The most conspicuous thing about DeKalb Junction in those days, aside from the red brick Goulding House, was the huge wood-shed and wood-pile beyond the small depot, which still stands there. It was customary for an engine to "wood up" at Watertown—in those days as in these again, all trains changed engines at Watertown—and again at DeKalb Junction before finishing her run into Ogdensburgh. Similarly upon the return trip, she would stop again at DeKalb to fill her tender; which, in turn, would carry her back to Watertown once again. Wood went all too quickly. I remember, sometime in the mid-eighties, riding from Prescott to Ottawa, upon the old Ottawa and St. Lawrence Railroad, and the wood-burner stopping somewhere between those towns to appease its seemingly insatiable appetite.

The wood-burners upon the R. W. & O. began to disappear sometime about the beginnings of the seventies. Apparently the first engine to have her fire-boxes changed to permit of the use of soft coal was the C. Comstock, which was rapidly followed by the Phelps, the Lord and the Alexander. They then had the extension boilers and the straight "diamond" stacks. A red band ran around the under flare of the diamond. About that time the road began adding to its motive power; new engines, among them the Theodore Irwin and the C. Zabriskie, were being purchased, and these were all coal burners, bituminous, of course. When, as we shall see, in a following chapter, the Syracuse Northern was merged into the R. W. & O., eight new locomotives were added to the growing fleet of the parent road; four Hinckleys and four Bloods.

Even at that time the road was beginning, although in a modest and somewhat hesitant way, the construction of its own locomotives in its own shops. William Jackson, the Master Mechanic there in 1873, built the J. W. Moak and the J. S. Farlow, both of them coal-burners for passenger service. He was succeeded by Abraham Close who built the Cataract and the Lewiston, and the Moses Taylor, too, in 1877. The following year the late George H. Hazleton was to become the road's Master Mechanic and so to remain as long as it retained its corporate existence.

In later years there were to come those famous Mogul twins, the Samson and the Goliath. There were, as I recall it, still two others of these Moguls, the Energy and the Efficiency. In a still later time the road, robbed of its pleasant personal way of locomotive nomenclature and adopting a strictly impersonal method of denoting its engines by serial numbers alone, was to take another forward step and bring in still larger Moguls; the "1," "2," "3," and "4."

But I anticipate. I cannot close this chapter without one more reference to my good friend, Frank W. Smith. He was an energetic little fellow; and after some twenty months of engine wiping there at Coffeen Street, and all the abuse and cuffing and chaffing that went with it, he won an honest promotion to the job of a locomotive fireman. It was a real job, real responsibility and real pay, thirty-nine dollars a month. Yet this job faded when he became an engineer. Job envied of all other jobs. How the boys would crowd around the Norris Woodruff at Adams depot, at Gouverneur, and all the rest of the way along the line and feast their eyes upon Frank Smith up there in the neat cab, that so quickly came to look like home to him! Fifty dollars a month pay! Overtime? Of course not. Agreements? Once more, no. This was nearly fifteen years ahead of that day when the engineers upon the Central Railroad of New Jersey were to formulate the first of these perplexing things.

But a good engine, a good job and good pay. They had the pleasant habit of assigning a crew to a definite engine in those days, and that piece of motive power invariably became their pet and pride. A good job was not only an honest one, but one of a considerable distinction. And fifty dollars a month was not bad pay, when cheese was eight cents a pound and butter seven, and a kind friend apt to give you all the eggs that you could take home in the top of your hat. Remuneration, in its last analysis is forever a comparative thing—and nothing more.

CHAPTER VI
THE R. W. & O. PROSPERS—AND EXPANDS

IN the mid-seventies the young city of Watertown was entering upon a rare era in which culture and great prosperity were to be blended. The men who walked its pleasant maple-shaded streets were real men, indeed: the Flower brothers—George W., Anson R. and Roswell P.—George B. Phelps, Norris Winslow, the Knowlton brothers—John C. and George W.—Talcott H. Camp, George A. Bagley, these were the men who were the town's captains of industry of that day. An earlier generation had passed away; Norris Woodruff, O. V. Brainard, Orville Hungerford; these men had played their large parts in the upbuilding of Watertown and were gone or else living in advanced years. A new generation of equal energy and ability had come to replace them. Roswell P. Flower was upon the threshold of that remarkable career in Wall Street that was to make him for a time its leader and give him the large political honor of becoming Governor of the State of New York. His brother, George W., first Mayor of Watertown, was tremendously interested in each of the city's undertakings. George B. Phelps had risen from the post of Superintendent of the old Potsdam & Watertown to be one of the town's richest men. He had a city house in New York—a handsome "brownstone front" in one of the "forties"—and in his huge house in Stone Street, Watertown, the luxury of a negro valet, John Fletcher, for many years a familiar figure upon the streets of the town.

From the pulpit of the dignified First Presbyterian Church in Washington Street, the venerable Dr. Isaac Brayton had now retired; his place was being filled by Dr. Porter, long to be remembered in the annals of that society. Dr. Olin was about entering old Trinity, still in Court Street. Into the ancient structure of the Watertown High School, in State Street, the genial and accomplished William Kerr Wickes was coming as principal. The Musical Union was preparing for its record run of Pinafore in Washington Hall. And in the old stone cotton factory on Beebee's Island, Fred Eames was tinkering with his vacuum air brake, little dreaming of the tragic fate that was to await him but a few years later; more likely, perhaps, of the great air brake industry to which he was giving birth and which, three decades later, was to take its proper place among the town's chief industries. Paper manufacturing, as it is known to-day in the North Country, was then a comparatively small thing; there were few important mills outside of those of the Knowltons or the Taggarts—the clans of

Remington, of Herring, of Sherman and of Anderson were yet to make their deep impress upon the community.

Carriage making was then a more important business than that of paper making. The very thought of the motor-car was as yet unborn and Watertonians reckoned the completion of a new carriage in the town in minutes rather than in hours. It made steam engines and sewing machines. All in all it created a very considerable traffic for its railroad—in reality for its railroads, for in 1872 a rival line had come to contest the monopoly of the Rome, Watertown & Ogdensburgh; of which more in good time.

As went Watertown, so went the rest of the North Country. It was a brisk, prosperous land, where industry and culture shared their forces. There was a plenitude of manufacturing even outside of Watertown, whilst the mines at Keene and Rossie had reopened and were shipping a modest five or six cars a day of really splendid red ore. People worked well, people thought well. The excellent seminaries at Belleville, at Adams, at Antwerp and at Gouverneur reflected a general demand for an education better than the public schools of that day might offer. The young St. Lawrence University up at Canton, after a hard beginning fight, was at last on its way to its present day strength and influence.

Northern New Yorkers traveled. They traveled both far and near. Even distant Europe was no sealed book to them. There were dozens of fine homes, even well outside of the towns and villages, which boasted their Steinway pianos and whose young folk, graduated from Yale or Mount Holyoke, spoke intelligently with their elders of Napoleon III or of the charms of the boulevards of Paris.

In the upbuilding of this prosperous era the Rome, Watertown & Ogdensburgh had played its own large part. By 1875 it was nearly a quarter of a century old. It was indeed an extremely high grade and prosperous property, the pride, not only of Watertown, which had been so largely responsible for its construction, but indeed of the entire North Country. It had, as we have already seen, as far back as 1866, succeeded in thrusting a line into Oswego, thirty miles west of Richland. After which it felt that it needed an entrance into Syracuse, then as now, a most important railroad center. To accomplish this entrance it leased, in 1875, the Syracuse Northern Railroad, and then gained at last a firm two-footed stand upon the tremendous main line of the New York Central & Hudson River Railroad. It continued to maintain, of course, its original connection at Rome—its long stone depot there still stands to-day, although far removed from the railroad tracks. Yet one, in memory at least, may see it as the brisk business place of yore, with the four tracks of the Vanderbilt trail curving upon the one side of it and the brightly painted yellow cars of the R. W. & O. waiting upon the other. The Rome connection gave the road direct access to Boston, New York, and to the East generally; that at Syracuse made the journey from Northern New York to western points much easier and more direct, than it had been through the Rome gateway. It was logical and it was strategic. And it is possible that had the Rome, Watertown & Ogdensburgh been content to remain satisfied with its system as it then existed, a good deal of railroad history that followed after, would have remained unwritten.

The railroad scheme that finally led to the building of the Syracuse Northern had been under discussion since 1851, the year of the completion of the Watertown & Rome Railroad. Yet, largely because of the paucity of good sized intermediate towns upon the lines of the proposed route, the plan for a long time had languished. In the late sixties it was successfully revived, however, and the Syracuse Northern Railroad incorporated, early in 1870, with a capital stock of $1,250,000 and the following officers:

President, ALLEN MUNROE

Secretary, PATRICK H. AGAN

Treasurer, E. B. JUDSON

Engineer, A. C. POWELL

Directors

Allen Munroe, Syracuse	Jacob S. Smith, Syracuse
E. W. Leavenworth, Syracuse	Horace K. White, Syracuse
E. B. Judson, Syracuse	Elizur Clark, Syracuse
Patrick Lynch, Syracuse	Garret Doyle, Syracuse
Frank H. Hiscock, Syracuse	William H. Canter, Brewerton
John A. Green, Syracuse	James A. Clark, Pulaski

Orin R. Earl, Sandy Creek

The road once organized found a lively demand for its shares. Its largest investor was the city of Syracuse, which subscribed for $250,000 worth of its bonds. The first depot of the new line in the city that gave it its birth was in Saxon Street, up in the old town of Salina. From there it was that Denison, Belden & Company began the construction of the railroad. It was not a difficult road to build, easy grades and but three bridges—a small one at Parish and two fairly sizable ones at Brewerton and at Pulaski—to go up, so it was finished and opened for traffic in the fall of 1871—which was precisely the same year that the New York Central opened its wonderful Grand Central Depot down on Forty-second Street, New York. The line ran through from Syracuse to Sandy Creek, now Lacona. It started off in good style, operating two passenger express trains, an accommodation and two freights each day in each direction. At the beginning it made a brave showing for itself, and soon after it was open it built for itself a one-storied brick passenger station across from the New York Central's, then new, depot in Syracuse, and at right angles to it. That station still stands but is now used as the Syracuse freight station of the American Railway Express.

E. H. Bancroft was the first superintendent of the Syracuse Northern, C. C. Morse, the second, and J. W. Brown, the third. J. Dewitt Mann was the accounting officer and paymaster. The road never attained to a long official roster of its own, however. Within a twelvemonth after its opening the prosperous Rome, Watertown & Ogdensburgh, having already seen the advantages of a two-footed connection with the New York Central, planned its purchase. The Syracuse road, having failed to become the financial success of which its promoters had hoped, this act was easily accomplished. The Sheriff of Onondaga County assisted. In 1875 there was a foreclosure sale and the Syracuse Northern ceased to live thereafter, save as a branch to Pulaski. A few years later the six miles of track between that town and Sandy Creek were torn up and abandoned. The old road-bed is still in plain sight, however, for a considerable distance along the line of the state highway to Watertown as it leads out of Pulaski, while the abutments of the former high railroad bridge over the Salmon River still show conspicuously in that village.

With its system fairly well rounded out, the Rome, Watertown & Ogdensburgh began the intensive perfection of its service. It built, in 1874, the first section of the long stone freight-house opposite the passenger station—so long a landmark of Watertown—from stone furnished by Lawrence Gage, of Chaumont. Mr. Moak, the Superintendent of the road at that time, was criticized for this expenditure. As a matter of fact it was necessary not only to twice enlarge it quite radically, but to build a relief transfer station at the Junction before the stone freight-house was finally torn down to make room for the present passenger station at Watertown.

Between the old freight-shed and the old passenger station there ran for many years but a single passenger track, curving all the way, and beside it the long platform, which was protected from the elements by a canopy, which in turn, had a canopied connection with the waiting-room; at that time still in the wing or original portion of the station; the main or newer portion, being occupied by the restaurant, which had passed from the hands of Col. Dunton into those of Silas Snell, Watertown's most famous cornet player of that generation.

At Watertown the Cape Vincent train would lay in at the end of the freight-house siding, and, because the Coffeen Street crossover had not then been constructed, would back in and out between the passenger station and the Watertown Junction, a little over a mile distant. Watertown Junction was still a point of considerable passenger importance. Long platforms were placed between the tracks there and passengers destined through to the St. Lawrence never went up into the main passenger station at all, but changed at that point to the Cape train.

The Thousand Islands were beginning to be known as a summer resort of surpassing excellence. The famous Crossmon House at Alexandria Bay was already more than two decades old. O. G. Staples had just finished that nine-days-wonder, the Thousand Island House, and plans were in the making for the building of the Round Island Hotel (afterwards the Frontenac) and other huge hostelries that were to make social history at the St. Lawrence, even before the coming of the cottage and club-house era.

It will be recalled that from the first the R. W. & O. developed excellent docking facilities at Cape Vincent. At the outset it had builded the large covered passenger station upon the wharf there, whose tragic destruction we have already witnessed. Beyond this were the freight-sheds and the grain elevator. For Cape Vincent's importance in those days was by no means limited to the passenger travel, which there debouched from the trains to take the steamers to the lower river points, or even that which all the year around made its tedious way across the broad river to Kingston, twenty-two miles away.

The Lady of the Lake passed out of existence some six or seven years after the inauguration of the Kingston ferry in connection with the trains into the Cape. She was replaced by the steamer Pierrepont—the first of this name—which was built on Wolfe Island in the summer of 1856 and went into service in the following spring. In that same summer of 1857 the canal was dug through the waistline girth of Wolfe Island, and a short and convenient route established through it, between Cape Vincent and

Kingston—some twelve or thirteen miles all told, as against nearly twice that distance around either the head or the foot of the island.

It was a pleasant ride through the old Wolfe Island canal. I can easily remember it, myself, the slow and steady progress of the steamboat through the rich farmlands and truck-gardens, the neatly whitewashed highway bridges, swinging leisurely open from time to time to permit of our progress. It is a great pity that the ditch was ever abandoned.

The first Pierrepont was not a particularly successful craft and it was supplemented in 1864 by the Watertown, which gradually took the brunt of the steadily increasing traffic across the St. Lawrence at this point. The ferry grew steadily to huge proportions and for many years a great volume of both passengers and freight was handled upon it. It is a fact worth noting here, perhaps, that the first through shipment of silk from the Orient over the newly completed transcontinental route of the Canadian Pacific Railway was made into New York, by way of the Cape Vincent ferry and the R. W. & O. in the late fall of 1883.

With the business of this international crossing steadily increasing, it became necessary to keep two efficient steamers upon the route and so the second Pierrepont was builded, going into service in 1874. At about that time the Watertown ceased her active days upon the river and the lake and was succeeded by the staunch steamer Maud. Here was a staunch craft indeed, built upon the Clyde somewhere in the late fifties or the early sixties, and shipped in sections from Glasgow to Montreal, where she was set up for St. Lawrence service, in which she still is engaged, under the name of the America. Her engines for many years were of a peculiar Scotch pattern, by no means usual in this part of the world, and apparently understood by no one other than Billy Derry, for many years her engineer. Occasionally Derry would quarrel with the owners of the Maud and quit his job. They always sent their apologies after him, however. No one else could run the boat, and they were faced with the alternative of bowing to his whims or laying up the steamer.

Yet, as I have already intimated, the passenger traffic was but a small part of Cape Vincent's importance through three or four great decades. The ferry carried mail, freight and express as well—the place was ever an important ferry crossing, a seat of a custom house of the first rank. In summer the steamer acted as ferry, for many years crossing the Wolfe Island barrier four times daily, through three or four miles of canal, which some time along in the early nineties was suffered to fill up and was abandoned in 1892. In midwinter mail and freight and passengers alike crossed in speed and a real degree of fine comfort in great four-horse sleighs upon a hard roadway of thick, thick ice. It was between seasons, when the ice was either forming or breaking and sleighs as utter an impossibility as steamboats that the real problem arose. In those times of the year a strange craft, which was neither sled nor boat, but a combination of both, was used. It went through the water and over the ice. Yet the result was not as easy as it sounds. More than one passenger paid his dollar to go from Cape Vincent to Kingston, for the privilege of pushing the heavy hand sled-boat over the ice, getting his feet wet in the bargain.

Into the many vagaries of North Country weather, I shall not enter at this time. In a later chapter we shall give some brief attention to them. It is enough here to say that a man who could fight a blizzard, coming in from off Ontario, and keep the line open could run a railroad anywhere else in the world. In after years I was to see, myself, some of these rare old fights; Russell plows getting into the drifts over their necks around-about Pulaski and Richland and Sandy Creek, seemingly half the motive power off the track. Yet these were no more than the road has had since almost the very day of its inception.

Once, in the midwinter of 1873, we had a noble old wind—the North Country has a way of having noble old winds, even to-day—and the huge spire of the First Presbyterian Church in Washington Street, Watertown, came tumbling down into the road, smashed into a thousand bits, and seemingly with no more noise than the sharp slamming of a blind.

That night—it was the evening of the fifteenth of January—the railroad in and about Watertown nearly collapsed. Trains were hugely delayed and many of them abandoned. The Watertown Times of the next day, naïvely announced:

"Conductor Sandiforth didn't come home last night and missed a good deal by not coming. He spent the evening with a party of shovelers working his way from Richland to Pierrepont Manor. Conductor Aiken followed him up with the night train but he couldn't pass him, and so both trains arrived here at 9:30 this (Thursday) morning."

Here Conductor Lew Sandiforth first comes into our picture and for a moment I shall interrupt my narrative to give a bit of attention to him. He is well worth the interruption of any narrative. We had many pretty well-known conductors on the old R. W. & O.—but none half so well-known as Lew Sandiforth. He was the wit of the old line, and its pet beau. It was said of him, that if there was a good looking woman on the afternoon train up to Watertown, Lew would quit taking tickets somewhere north of Sandy

Creek. The train then could go to the Old Harry for all he cared. He had his social duties to perform. He was not one to shirk such responsibilities.

In those days a railroad conductor was something of an uncrowned king, anyway. His pay was meager, but ofttimes his profits were large. One of these famous old ticket punchers upon the Rome road lived at the Woodruff House, in Watertown, throughout the seventies. His wage was seventy-five dollars a month, but he paid ninety dollars a month board for his wife and himself and kept a driver and a carriage in addition. No questions were asked. The road, on the whole, was glad to get its freight and its ticket office revenues. Even these last were nothing to brag about. It was a poor sort of a public man in those days who could not have his wallet lined with railroad annual passes. A large proportion of the passengers upon the average train rode free of any charge. Sometimes this attained a scandalous volume. Away back in 1858, I find the Directors of the Potsdam & Watertown resolving that no officer of their company "shall give a free pass for more than one trip over the road to any one person, except officers of other railroad companies; and that an account of all free passes taken up shall be entered by the conductors in their daily returns with the name of the person passed and the name of the person who gave the pass, and the Superintendent shall submit statement thereof to each meeting of the Board." Moreover, he was requested to notify the conductors not to pass any persons without a pass except the Directors and Secretary of the company, and their families, the roadmaster, paymaster, station agents, and "persons who the conductors think are entitled to charity."

Despite obstacles to its full earning power such as this, the Rome, Watertown & Ogdensburgh prospered ... and progressed. Forever it was planning new frills to add to its operation. In 1865 it had placed a through Wagner sleeping-car in service between Watertown and New York. In 1875 this was an established function, leaving Watertown on the 6:30 train each evening and arriving in New York at 7:55 the next morning; returning it left New York each evening at six, and Albany at 11:40, and was in Watertown at 9:05 the next morning. A later management of the R. W. & O. in a fit of economy discontinued this service, and for more than twenty years the North Country stood in line for sleeping-car berths at Utica station, while it fought for the restoration of its sleeping-cars. These cars eventually came back, but not regularly until 1891, when the New York Central took over the property and put its up-to-date traffic methods upon it once again.

The local management of the mid-seventies—composed almost entirely of Watertown men—was not content to stop with the through sleeping cars between their chief town and New York. They finally instructed H. H. Sessions, their Master Mechanic, down in the old shops at Rome, to build two wonderful new cars for their line, "the likes of which had never been seen before." Mr. Sessions approached his new task with avidity. He was a born car-builder, in after years destined to take charge of the motive power department of the International & Great Northern Railway, at Palestine, Texas, and then, in January, 1887, to become Manager of the great Pullman car works at Pullman, Ill., just outside of Chicago. For six years he held this position, afterwards resigning it to enter into business for himself. The first vestibuled trains in which the platforms were enclosed, were built under his supervision under what are known to-day as the "Sessions Patents." He was indeed an inventive genius, and also designed the first steel platforms and other very modern devices in progressive car construction.

Sessions produced two sleeping-cars for the old Rome road. The "likes of them" had never been seen before, and never will be seen again. They were named the St. Lawrence and the Ontario, and, despite the fact that they depended upon candle-light as their sole means of illumination, they were wonderfully finished in the rarest of hard-woods. Alternately they were sleeping-cars and parlor-cars. At the first they were distinguished by the fact that they possessed no upper-berths, their mattresses, pillows and linen being carried in closets at either end of the car.

These cars at one time were placed in service between Syracuse, Watertown and Fabyan's, N. H., passing enroute through Norwood, Rouse's Point and Montpelier. One of them was in charge of Ed. Frary, the son of the General Ticket Agent of the R. W. & O. at that time, and the other in charge of L. S. Hungerford, who originally came from Evan's Mills. This was the Hungerford, who to-day is Vice-President and General Manager of the Pullman Company, at Chicago. A third or "spare" car was afterwards purchased from the Pullman Company and renamed the DeKalb.

Because of the limited carrying capacity of these R. W. & O. sleeping-cars they were never profitable. They did a little better when they were in day service as parlor-cars. One of Mr. Richard Holden's most vivid memories is of one of these cars coming into Watertown from the south on the afternoon train, which would halt somewhere near the Pine Street cutting to slip it off, preparatory to placing it on the Cape train at the Junction.

"I remember," he says, "how proud the late Frank Cornish was in riding down the straight on the first drawing-room car, with his hands on the brakewheel. He was a brakeman at that time. Afterwards he was promoted to baggageman and then to conductor, having the run on Number One and

Number Seven for many years, afterwards conducting a cigar-stand in the Yates Hotel at Syracuse until he died."

When hard times came upon the Rome, Watertown & Ogdensburgh these cars were laid up. Once in later years, under the Parsons management, they were renamed the Cataract and the Niagara, and operated in the Niagara Falls night trains. But again, they proved too much of a financial drag, and they were finally converted into day-coaches. There was another parlor-car, the Watertown. Eventually this became the private-car of Mr. H. M. Britton, General Manager of the R. W. & O., while the others remained day coaches; still retaining, however, their wide plate-glass windows and their general appearance of comfortable ease.

Here indeed was the golden age of the Rome road. Its bright, neat, yellow cars, its smartly painted and trimmed engines all bespoke the existence of a prosperous little rail carrier, that might have left well enough alone. But, seemingly it could not. There is a man living in the western part of this state, who recalls one fine day there in the mid-seventies, when Mr. Massey—the President of the road, came walking out of the Watertown station, talking all the time to Mr. Moak, its General Superintendent—came over to him:

"We're going to be a real railroad at last, John," said he. "We're going through to Niagara Falls upon our own rails and get into the trunk-line class."

He was giving expression to a dream of years. A moment ago and we were speaking of the operation through two or three summers of sleeping-cars between Watertown and the White Mountains over the R. W. & O., the Northern (at that time, already become the Ogdensburgh & Lake Champlain), the Central Vermont, the Montpelier and Wells River, and the Portland and Ogdensburgh. The officers of the Rome road felt that, if they could bridge the gap existing between the terminals of their line at Oswego, and go through to Suspension Bridge or Buffalo, where there were plenty of competing lines through to Chicago and the West, that they could both enter upon the competitive business of carrying western freight to the Atlantic seaboard, and at the same time stand independent of the New York Central. Eventually their idea was to take a concrete form, but again I anticipate.

In that brisk day there was, in the slow and laborious process of building a railroad, leading due west from Oswego. It was called the Lake Ontario Shore Railroad, and its construction was indeed a laborious process. For many years it came to an end just eighteen miles beyond Oswego. Finally it reached the little village of Ontario, fifty-one miles beyond. And there stopped dead. If it had forever been halted there, it would have been a good thing. Its promoters were both industrious and persistent, however. They chose to overlook the fact that the narrow territory, that they sought to thread, promised small local traffic returns for many years to come; a thin strip it was between the main line of the New York Central and the south shore of Lake Ontario, and although nearly 150 miles in length, never more than twelve or fifteen in width, and without any sizable communities. The prospect of a profitable traffic, originating in so thin a strip, was small indeed.

The prospectors of the Lake Ontario Shore Railroad did not see it that way. They stressed the fact that at Sterling they would intersect the Southern Central (now the Lehigh Valley), at Sodus the Northern Central (now the Pennsylvania), at Charlotte; the port of Rochester, the Rochester & State Line (now the Buffalo, Rochester & Pittsburgh) all in addition to the many valuable connections to be made at the Niagara River. Yet for a considerable time after the road had been pushed through Western New York, it came to a dead stop at Lewiston. Its original terminal can still be seen in that small village.

It was then thought possible and feasible to build a railroad bridge across the Niagara and the international boundary between Lewiston and Queenstown, in competition with the Suspension Bridge, which from the very moment of its opening in 1849 had been an overwhelming success. The energetic group of Oswego men who had promoted the building of the Lake Ontario Shore, hoped to duplicate the success of the Suspension Bridge there at Lewiston. They saw that small frontier New York town transformed into a real railroad metropolis.

"And what a line we shall have, running right up to it!" they argued. "Seventy-three out of our seventy-six miles, west of the Genesee River, as straight as the proverbial ruler-edge; and a maximum gradient of but twenty-six feet to the mile! What opportunities for fast—and efficient operation!"

They had capitalized their line at $4,000,000 and in October, 1870, when I first find official mention of it, they had expended $54,300 upon it. Its officers at that time were:

President, GILBERT MOLLISON, Oswego

Treasurer, LUTHER WRIGHT, Oswego

Secretary, HENRY L. DAVIS, Oswego

Engineer, ISAAC S. DOANE, Oswego

Directors

Luther Wright, Oswego	Oliver P. Scovell, Lewiston
Alanson S. Page, Oswego	George I. Post, Fairhaven
Fred'k T. Carrington, Oswego	William O. Wood, Red Creek
Gilbert Mollison, Oswego	Burt Van Horne, Lockport
Reuben F. Wilson, Wilson	James Brackett, Rochester
Joseph L. Fowler, Ransonville	D. F. Worcester, Rochester

It is needless to say that the railroad bridge was never thrust across the Niagara at Lewiston. That project died "a'borning." And so, almost, did the Lake Ontario Shore Railroad. As I have just said, the building of the road finally was halted at Ontario, fifty-one miles west of Oswego. Finally, by tremendous effort and the injection of some capital from the wealthy city of Rochester into the project it was brought through in 1875 as far as Kendall, a miserable little railroad, wretched and woe-begone with its sole rolling stock consisting of two second-hand locomotives, two passenger-cars and some fifty or sixty freight-cars.

In the long run, just as most folk had anticipated from the beginning, it was the wealthy and prosperous Rome, Watertown & Ogdensburgh that took over the Lake Ontario Shore and completed it; in 1876 as far as Lewiston, and a year or two later up the face of the Niagara escarpment to Suspension Bridge and the immensely valuable connections there. The merger, itself, was consummated in the midsummer of 1875. To reach the tracks of the new connecting link, from those of the old road, it was necessary not only to build an exceedingly difficult little tunnel under the hill, upon which the Oswego Court House stands, but to bridge the wide expanse of the river just beyond, a tedious and expensive process, which occupied considerably more than a twelvemonth.

All of this was not done until 1876 and by that time disaster threatened. The Rome road had gone quite too far. Times were growing very hard once again. A tight money market threatened; the storm of '73 had been passed but that of '77 was still ahead. It began to be a question whether the R. W. & O. could weather the large obligations that it had assumed when it had absorbed the Lake Ontario Shore. Traffic did not come off the new line; not, at least, in any considerable or profitable quantities. It defaulted on the interest payments of its bonds.

There was the beginning of disaster. The Rome road management realized this. They cut their dividends a little, and then to nothing. Watertown was staggered. For a long term of years up to 1870 the road had paid its ten per cent annual dividend with astonishing regularity. In that year it dropped a little—to eight per cent—the next year, to seven, and then in the panic year of 1873 to but three and one-half. The following year it had returned, with increasing good times, to seven. In the fiscal year of 1874-75 the Directors of the property had voted six and one-half. That was the end. The cancer of the Lake Ontario Shore was upon the parent property. The strong old R. W. & O. had permitted the default of the interest payments upon the bonds of their leased property. Confusion ruled among the men in the depot at Watertown. They were dazed with impending disaster.

CHAPTER VII
INTO THE SLOUGH OF DESPOND

THE enthusiasm which Mr. Marcellus Massey showed over the extension of his railroad into Suspension Bridge was surface enthusiasm, indeed. In his heart he felt that it had taken a very dangerous step. His mind was full of forebodings. Some of these he confessed to his intimates in Watertown. He felt that a mistake—if you please, an irrevocable mistake—had been made. And there was no turning back.

These forebodings were realized. As we have just seen, the Lake Ontario Shore defaulted upon its bonds in 1876 and again in 1877. The reflection of this disastrous step came directly upon the R. W. & O. It ceased paying dividends. The North Country folk, who had come to regard its securities as something hardly inferior to government bonds, were depressed and then alarmed. Yet worse was to come. On August 1, 1878, the R. W. & O. defaulted in its interest on its great mass of consolidated bonds.

The blow had fallen! Failure impended! And receivership! Yet, in the long run, both were avoided. Into the directorate of the railroad, up to that time a fairly close Northern New York affair, a new man had come. He was a smallish man, with a reputation for keenness and sagacity in railroad affairs, second only to that of Jay Gould or Daniel Drew. There were more ways than one in which Samuel Sloan, known far and wide as plain "Sam Sloan," resembled both of these men.

His touch with the R. W. & O. came physically, by way of the contact of the Delaware, Lackawanna and Western with it at three points; at Oswego, at Syracuse, and at Rome—this last, at that time through its leased operation of the Rome & Clinton Railroad, which ceased July 1, 1883. He had looked upon the development and the despair of the Rome road with increasing interest. His careful and conservative mind must have stood aghast at the foolhardiness of the Lake Ontario Shore venture. Sam Sloan would have done nothing of that sort. The railroad that he dominated so forcefully for many years—Lackawanna—would have taken no step of that sort. Trust Sam Sloan for that.

And yet, despite his evident dislike for the property, the R. W. & O. had its fascinations for him. He must have seen certain opportunities in it. The fact that it touched his own road at so many points, and, therefore, was capable of becoming so large a potential feeder for it—despite the malign influence of those Vanderbilts with their important New York Central—must have appealed to the old man's heart. At any rate he took direct steps to gain control of the Rome road.

The precise motives that impelled Samuel Sloan to gain a control of the R. W. & O., and having once gained a control of it, to conduct it in the remarkable manner that he did, in all probability, never will be known. One may only indulge in surmises. But just why he should seek, apparently with deliberateness and carefully preconceived plan, to wreck what had been so recently the finest of all railroads in the state of New York is not clearly apparent even to-day.

Sloan was a man of many moods. Receptive and interested to-day, he was cold and bitter to-morrow. One might never count upon him. He flattered Marcellus Massey, raised his salary as the President of the Rome road from $7500 to $10,000 a year, and then induced him to purchase large holdings of Lackawanna stock, putting up as collateral his large holdings of the shares of the R. W. & O., just beginning their long drop towards a pitifully low figure—all the time holding the bait to the old President of the amazing property that he was about to upbuild in Northern New York. So, eventually Sloan ruined Massey, financially and physically, and a broken hearted man went out from the old President's office of the R. W. & O. in Watertown.

In 1877, the year before the Rome road all but created financial disaster in Northern New York, Sloan had bought enough of its bargain-sale stock to have himself elected as its President. The official roster of the road then became:

    President, SAMUEL SLOAN, New York

    Vice-President, MARCELLUS MASSEY, Watertown

    Treasurer, J. A. LAWYER, Watertown

    General Freight Agent, E. M. MOORE, Watertown

    General Ticket Agent, H. T. FRARY, Watertown

    Supt. R. W. & O. Division, J. W. MOAK, Watertown

    Supt. L. O. & S. N. Division, E. A. VAN HORNE, Oswego

Directors

Marcellus Massey, Watertown Moses Taylor, Scranton

Samuel Sloan, New York		C. Zabriskie, New York

William E. Dodge, New York	John S. Barnes, New York

John S. Farlow, Boston		S. D. Hungerford, Adams

Percy R. Pyne, New York		Gardner R. Colby, New York

Talcott H. Camp, Watertown	William M. White, Utica

Theodore Irwin, Oswego

The North Country complexion of the directorate had all but disappeared. As far back as 1871, Addison Day had ceased to be Superintendent of the road, and had become Superintendent of the Utica & Black River. He had been succeeded by J. W. Moak, a former roadmaster of the Rome road. Moak was not only equally as efficient as Day, but he was much more popular, both with the road's employees and its patrons. Yet one of Sloan's first acts was to relieve him of a portion of his territory and responsibility. He made the point, and it was not without force, that it was all but impossible for an operating officer at Watertown to supervise properly the western end of the now far-flung system. So, he took the former Syracuse Northern, the Lake Ontario Shore and the branch from Richland to Oswego—all the lines west of Richland, in fact—and made them into a new division, with headquarters at Oswego. For this division he brought one of his few favored officers from the Lackawanna, E. A. Van Horne, who had been a Superintendent upon that property. Van Horne was a forceful man, who, as he went upward, made a distinct impress upon the railroad history of the North Country. He was quick tempered, decisive, yet possessing certain very likable qualities that were of tremendous help to him there.

Another of Sloan's early acts—more easily understood than some others—was to tear out the soft-coal grates of the fire boxes of the R. W. & O. locomotives, and substitute for them hard-coal grates. Anthracite then, as now, was a great specialty of the Lackawanna. And in the road to the north of him Sloan possessed a customer of no mean dimensions.

For the next four or five years the R. W. & O. grubbed along—and barely dodged receivership. Its service steadily went from bad to worse. It now took the best passenger trains upon the line four hours to go from Watertown to Rome, seventy-two miles (in the very beginnings of the road, they had done it in an even three hours). No one knew when a freight car would reach New York from Watertown. Confusion reigned. Chaos was at hand. And when Watertown merchants and manufacturers would go to

Oswego to protest to Mr. Van Horne (Mr. Moak finally had been demoted, and Watertown suffered the humiliation of having the operating headquarters of the system moved away from it) they would hear from the General Superintendent of the property his utter helplessness in the matter; the threats from Sloan were that he might close down the road altogether, and Van Horne was beside himself for explanations:

"Gentlemen, I cannot do better," he said, over and over again, "our track is in deplorable condition. I dare not send a train over the road without sending a man afoot, station to station, ahead of it to make sure that the rails will hold."

So it was. The track inspectors' jobs were cut out for them these days. They made some long-distance walking records. Yet, despite their vigilance, train wrecks came with increasing frequency. Morale was gone. The fine old R. W. & O. was at the bottom of the Slough of Despond. Added to all this were the rigors of a North Country winter, which we are to see in some detail in another chapter. According to the veracious diary of Moses Eames, on January 2nd, 1879, the first train came into Watertown since Christmas Day. The following day it snowed again, and fiercely and the R. W. & O. went out of business for another ten days. That storm was almost a record-breaker: more than a fortnight of continuous snow and extreme low temperature.

In those days Samuel Sloan was busy occupying himself with an extension of his beloved Lackawanna into Buffalo. That, in itself, was a real job. For years the D. L. & W. had terminated at Great Bend, a few miles east of Binghamton, and had used trackage rights upon the Erie from there West, not only into the Buffalo gateway, but also to reach its branch-line properties into Utica, Rome, Syracuse and Ithaca. Sloan finally had quarreled with the Erie—it was a way he ofttimes had. And, for once at least, had made a bold strategic move through to the far end of the Empire State.

To build so many miles of railroad one must have rail. And rail costs much money, unless one may borrow it from a friendly property. So Sloan went up into the North Country and "borrowed" rail. He "borrowed" so much that travel upon the R. W. & O. became fraught with many real dangers—and the life of his General Superintendent at Oswego, Van Horne, a nightmare. Some of the rails were, in his own words, not more than six feet long. Finally in desperation he appealed to his chief competitor in the North Country, the Utica & Black River, which rapidly was substituting steel for iron upon its main line. In sheer pity, J. F. Maynard, General

Superintendent of the Utica & Black River, sent his discarded iron to his paralyzed competitor.

There was little steel upon the Rome road in 1883—less than sixty miles of its 417 miles of main line track was so equipped. Neither were there sufficient locomotives; but fifty-two of them all-told, in addition to two or three that the Lackawanna had had the extreme kindness to "loan" the property—upon a perfectly adequate rental basis. Long since it had ceased to operate such frills as sleeping-cars or parlor-cars. It had only fifty-four passenger-coaches; not nearly enough to meet the needs of so far-flung a line. And many of these were in extreme disrepair. An elderly citizen of Ogdensburgh says that it was a nightly occasion for the R. W. & O. train to come in from DeKalb with more than half of its journals ablaze.

Yet, despite these bitter years, the road had managed to avoid receivership and in 1882 it succeeded in effecting a reorganization; under which it dropped the interest on its bonds to five per cent and assessed its stockholders ten dollars a share for a cash working fund to keep it alive. They were given income bonds for the amount so contributed by them. There were a few grumbles at this arrangement, but not many. The huge potential possibilities of the property—or rather of the rich and still undeveloped territory that it served—were too generally recognized.

It began to be rumored that new outside interests were buying into the stock in Wall Street. These rumors were brought to Sloan's attention.

"Look out," he was warned, "some one will get that old heap of junk away from you yet."

He laughed. At the best you could tell Samuel Sloan but little. Gradually, he proceeded with his reorganization, and in 1883 we find the official roster of the reorganized R. W. & O. reading in this fashion:

    President, SAMUEL SLOAN, New York

    Secretary and Treasurer, J. A. LAWYER, Watertown

    General Superintendent, E. A. VAN HORNE, Oswego

    Master Mechanic, G. H. HASELTON, Oswego

    General Ticket Agent, H. T. FRARY, Watertown

    General Freight Agent, E. M. MOORE, Oswego

Directors

Talcott H. Camp, Watertown	Charles Parsons, New York
S. D. Hungerford, Adams	Clarence S. Day, New York
William M. White, Utica	Percy R. Pyne, New York
Theodore Irwin, Oswego	John S. Barnes, New York
William E. Dodge, New York	John S. Farlow, Boston
Roswell G. Ralston, New York	Gardner R. Colby, New York

The rumor-mongers were not without fact to support them, for a new name will be noticed upon this list; that of Charles Parsons, of New York, who had been carefully garnering in R. W. & O. stock, at from ten to fifteen cents on the dollar. Two names had disappeared, those of Marcellus Massey and of J. W. Moak. But we focus our attention upon the name of Parsons, and then step forward in our narrative until the sixth day of June, 1883, when the Directors of the R. W. & O. held a meeting in the back room of the Jefferson County Bank in Watertown.

There was an unusually full attendance of the Board. Mr. Sloan, as was his prerogative through his office as President of the road, sat at the head of the long table. Near its foot sat Mr. Parsons, a cadaverous man, with prematurely white hair, given to much thought but little speech. The business of the meeting, the election of officers for the ensuing year, was perfunctory and quickly accomplished. The Secretary arose and announced that Mr. Parsons had been elected President of the R. W. & O. Sloan flushed, and then prepared to spring a coup d'etat. He brought a packet of papers from out of an inside pocket.

"What do you propose to do with these?" he snarled.

"What are they?" asked Parsons.

"Notes of the road for $300,000 that I've advanced it, to keep it out of bankruptcy," was the reply.

"Let me see them," said its new President.... He glanced at the papers for a moment, then reached for his check-book and wrote his check to Sloan for a clean $300,000. He handed it across the table. The retiring President scrutinized it sharply, placed it within his wallet and left the room. His connection with the road was terminated. At the best it was a sinister connection. There were few to regret his going.

With his hand firmly fixed upon its wheel, Parsons began the complete reorganization of his newly acquired property. He had his long-time associate, Clarence S. Day, elected as its Vice-President, and within a very few weeks had brought to the operating headquarters in Oswego a fine upstanding man, the late H. M. Britton, as General Manager of the road, a newly created title and office. Mr. Britton at once chose two operating lieutenants for himself; W. H. Chauncey, as Assistant Superintendent of the Western Division (west of Richland) at Oswego, and the famous "Jud" Remington, as Assistant Superintendent of the Eastern Division, at Watertown.

Watertown had hoped that with the new management of the road—that railroad which it had been prone to call "its road"—would reëstablish the operating headquarters of the property there, also new and enlarged shops. In these hopes it was to be doomed to great disappointment. For not only was a Sloan policy to consolidate shop facilities at Oswego continued and enlarged—the shops both at Rome and at Watertown were reduced to facilities for emergency repairs only—but the corporate executive offices were removed from it to New York City, while the chief operating headquarters of the company remained at Oswego.

Yet Watertown might easily enough take hope. The service upon the road was improved—at once. In front of me I have a copy of the shortlived Daily Republican, which once was printed there. It is dated, July 24, 1885, and its rules are turned to black borders of mourning in tribute to General Grant, who died upon the preceding day. In the lower corner of one of its pages is an advertisement of the summer service upon the R. W. & O. It was a real service, indeed—five trains a day over the main line in each direction, and adequate schedules upon the branches. In that season of the year there was through sleeping-car service between Watertown and New York, upon the sleeping-cars that were operated in and out of Cape Vincent to serve the steadily, increasing, tourist trade upon the St. Lawrence. The Parsons' management, however, like the Sloan, steadfastly refused to operate this sleeping-car service through the autumn, winter and spring months of the year. There was a through sleeping-car service, also, to the White Mountains, the car coming through from Niagara Falls, passing Watertown at four o'clock in the morning and reaching Fabyan's, N. H., at twenty-eight minutes after four in the afternoon; Portland, Me., by direct connection, at 8:25 p. m. This advertisement is signed by W. F. Parsons, as General Passenger Agent, and by Mr. Britton, as General Manager of the line.

Britton was alert to suggestion and to complaint. To favored persons he was apt to make an occasional suggestion upon the company's stock.

"Buy it now," he urged. "Buy it—and hold it."

Most folk shook their heads negatively at that suggestion. Watertown had been burned once in a railroad experience. It now emulated the traditional wise child. "Buy the stock," whispered Britton to a Watertown manufacturer. It then was at twenty-five. The Watertownian demurred. A year later it was forty. "Buy it now," Britton still whispered to him. And still our cautious soul of the North Country hesitated. It touched fifty. Britton still urged. Of course, the Watertown man would not buy it then. He prided himself that he never bought anything at the top of the market. Sixty, seventy, then R. W. & O. in the great market of Wall Street touched seventy-five.

"How about it now?" said Britton over the wire.

The Watertown man laughed. He had made a mistake—one of the few financial errors that he ever made—and he could afford to laugh at this one. Buy R. W. & O. at seventy-five? Not he. Let the other man do it. Afterwards he did not laugh as hard. He lived long enough to see R. W. & O. reach par once again—and then cross it and keep upwards all the while. He saw it reach 105, then 110 and then on a certain memorable March day in 1891, 123.

But this anticipates. We are riding too rapidly with our narrative. If old "Jud" Remington were traveling with us upon this special he would do, as sometimes was his wont, reach up and pull the bell-cord to slow the train. He took no risks, did "Jud"—bless his fine, old heart.

We have anticipated—and perhaps we have neglected. All these years, of which we have been writing, the R. W. & O. had a competitor—a very live competitor, we must have you understand. So live, that to gain a permanent position for itself, that competitor must needs be completely eliminated. To that competitor—the Utica & Black River Railroad—we must now turn our attention.

CHAPTER VIII
THE UTICA & BLACK RIVER

THE beginnings of the Utica & Black River Railroad go away back to 1852—the year of the real completion and opening of the Watertown & Rome. The fact that not only could that line be built successfully, but that there would come to it immediately a fine flow of traffic was not without its effect upon the staunch old city of Utica, which had felt rather bitterly about the loss, to its smaller neighbor, Rome, of the prestige of being the gateway city to the North Country. From the beginning Utica had been that gateway. Long ago we read of the fine records that were made on the old post-road from Utica through Martinsburgh and Watertown to Sackett's Harbor. The Black River valley was the logical pathway to the Northern Tier. The people who dwelt there felt that God had made it so. And now the infamy had come to pass that a new man-built highway had ignored it completely; had passed far to the west of it.

Spurred by such feelings, stung by a new-found feeling of isolation, the people of Lewis County held a mass meeting on a December evening in 1852, at Lowville, to which their county-seat had already been moved from Martinsburgh, but two miles distant. They set the fire to a popular feeling that already demanded a railroad through the natural easy gradients of the valley of the Black River. The blaze of indignation spread. Within a fortnight similar meetings were held at Boonville and at Theresa. And within a few months the Black River Railroad Company was organized at the first of these towns with a capital of $1,200,000 and Herkimer, in the valley of the Mohawk, was designated as its probably southern terminal.

Once again Utica writhed in civic anguish. But in three days gave answer to this proposed, second blow to her prestige by the organization of the Black River & Utica Railroad, with a capital of $1,000,000—a tentative figure of course. As an evidence of her good faith she raised a cash fund for the employment of Daniel C. Jenney to survey a route for her own railroad, north and straight through to French Creek (about to become the present village of Clayton) one hundred miles distant.

To this move Rome replied. Having acquired a new and exclusive prestige, she was quite unwilling that it should be lost, or even dimmed. She called attention to the fact that she was, in her own eyes, of course, the logical gateway to the Black River country, as well as to the eastern shore of Lake Ontario, to which the Watertown & Rome already led. There was a natural pass that rested just behind her that led to Boonville and the upper waters of the Black River. Had not this natural route been recognized some years before by the builders of the Black River Canal, who readily had chosen it for the waterway, which to this day remains in operation through it?

Rome felt that her argument was quite irrefutable. To support it, however, she pledged herself to furnish terminal grounds for the new line at $250 an acre, in addition to subscribing $450,000 to the stock and bonds of the company. Money talks. Utica came back with an offer of terminal lands at $200 an acre and proffered a subscription of $650,000 to the securities of the Black River & Utica. A meeting was held. The mooted question of a southern terminal was put to vote. Rome and Utica tied with twenty-two votes each; Herkimer, despite her suggestion of the valley of Canada Creek as a natural pathway for the new line north to the watershed of the Black River, had but two votes. She promptly withdrew from the contest.

Money does talk. Eventually Utica had the terminal of the Black River road, even though the noble Romans, retiring to their camp in a blue funk for a time threatened a rival line straight north from their town to Boonville and beyond. They went so far as to incorporate this company; as the Ogdensburgh, Clayton & Rome. The promoters of the Black River & Utica having planned to locate their line in the low levels of the flats of the river, the Rome group said that they would build their road upon the higher level, rather closely paralleling the ancient state highway and so making especial appeal to the towns along it, which felt miffed at the indifference of the Utica group to them.

In the long run, as we all know, the road was built along the low level of the Black River valley, and many of the once thriving towns along the State Road left stranded high and dry. The road from Rome became a memory. From time to time the suggestion has been revived, however—in my boyhood days we had the fine classical suggestion of the Rome & Carthage Railroad all ready for incorporation—but there is little prospect now that such a road will ever be built. The times are not propitious now for that sort of enterprise.

Ground was broken at Utica for the new Black River line on August 27, 1853. There was a deal of ceremony to the occasion; no less a personage than the distinguished Governor Horatio Seymour, being designated to make remarks appropriate to it. And, as was the custom in those days for such an event, there was a parade, music by the bands and other appropriate festivities. Construction, in the hands of Contractor J. S. T. Stranahan, of Brooklyn, went ahead with great briskness. Within two years the line had been builded over the hard rolling country of the upper Canada Creek—it included the crossing of a deep gully near Trenton Falls by a high trestle (subsequently replaced by a huge embankment)—to Boonville, thirty-five miles distant from Utica.

This much done, the Black River & Utica subsided and became apparently a semi-dormant enterprise—for a number of long years. The promises which its promoters had made to have the line completed to Clayton by the first of July, 1855, apparently were forgotten. These had been made at a mass meeting of the enthusiastic proponents of the Ogdensburgh, Clayton & Rome, held at Constableville on the evening of Monday, August 22, 1853. They were definite, and the Rome crowd under them badly worsted. But promises were as easily made in those days as in these. As easily accepted ... and as easily broken.

In 1857, the Black River & Utica Railroad was operating a single passenger train a day, between Utica and Boonville. It left Boonville at eight o'clock in the morning and arrived at Utica at 10:20 a. m. The return run left Utica at 4:00 p. m. and arrived at Boonville at 6:20 p. m. Seventy-five cents was charged to ride from Utica to Trenton and $1.25 from Utica to Boonville. The little road then had four locomotives, the T. S. Faxton, the J. Butterfield, the Boonville and the D. C. Jenney. The Faxton hauled the passenger train, and a young man from Boonville, who also owned a coalyard there, was its conductor. His name was Richard Marcy and afterwards he was to come to prominent position, not only as exclusive holder of its coal-selling franchise for a number of years, but also as a politician of real parts.

In 1858, the little road doubled its passenger service. Now there were two passenger trains a day in each direction. And each was at least fairly well-filled, for the Black River & Utica held as its supreme attraction Trenton Falls. Indeed, if it had not been for the prominence of Trenton Falls as a resort in those years, it is quite probable that a good many folk in the State of New York would never have even heard of it.

THE BIRTH OF THE U. & B. R.
The Boonville Passenger Train Standing in the Utica Station, Away Back in 1865.

But Trenton Falls—Trenton Falls of the sixties, of the fifties—all the way back to the late twenties, if you please—here was a place to be reckoned! All the great travelers of the early half of the last century—European as well as American—made a point of visiting it. The most of them wrote of it in their memoirs. That indefatigable tourist, N. P. Willis, could not miss this exquisitely beautiful place—alas, in these late days, the exquisitely beautiful place has fallen under the vandal hands of power engineers, and the exquisite beauty no longer is. Trenton Falls is but a memory. Yet the record of its one-time magnificence still remains.

"... The company of strangers at Trenton is made somewhat select by the expense and difficulty of access," wrote Willis, late in the fifties. The Black River & Utica had then barely been opened through to the Falls. "Most who come stay two or three days, but there are usually boarders here who stay for a longer time.... Nothing could be more agreeable than the footing upon which these chance-met residents and their daily accessions of newcomers pass their evenings and take strolls up the ravine together; and for those who love country air and romantic rambles without 'dressing for dinner' or waltzing by a band, this is 'a place to stay.' These are not the most numerous frequenters of Trenton, however. It is a very popular place of resort from every village within thirty miles; and from ten in the morning until four in the afternoon there is gay work with the country girls and their beaux—swinging under trees, strolling about in the woods near the house, bowling, singing, and dancing—at all of which (owing, perhaps to a certain gypsy-ish promiscuosity of my nature that I never could aristocrify by the keeping of better company) I am delighted to be, at least, a looker-on. The average number of these visitors from the neighborhood is forty or fifty a day, so that breakfast and tea are the nearest approach to 'dress meals'—the dinner, though profuse and dainty in its fare, being eaten in what is commonly thought to be rather 'mixed society.' I am inclined to think that, from French intermixture, or some other cause, the inhabitants of this region are a little peculiar in their manners. There is an unconsciousness or carelessness of others' observation and presence that I have hitherto seen only abroad. We have songs, duets and choruses, sung here by village girls, within the last few days, in a style that drew all in the house to listen very admiringly; and even the ladies all agree that there have been very pretty girls day after day among them. I find they are Fourierites to the extent of common hair-brush and other personal furniture—walking into anybody's room for the temporary repairs which belles require on their travels, and availing themselves of whatever was therein, with a simplicity, perhaps, a little transcendental. I had obtained the extra privilege for myself of a small dressing room apart, for which I presumed the various trousers and other merely masculine belongings would be protective scarecrows sufficient to keep out these daily female invaders, but, walking in yesterday, I found my combs and brushes in active employ, and two very tidy looking girls making themselves at home without shutting the door and no more disturbed by my entrée than if I had been a large male fly. As friends were waiting I apologized for intruding long enough to take a pair of boots from under their protection, but my presence was evidently no interruption. One of the girls (a tall figure, like a woman in two syllables connected by a hyphen at the waist) continued to look at the back of her dress in the glass, and the other went on threading her most prodigal chevelure with my doubtless very embarrassed though unresisting hair-brush, and so I abandoned the field, as of course I was expected to do ... I do not know that they would go to the length of 'fraternizing' one's tooth-brush, but with the exception of locking up that rather confidential article, I give in to the customs of the country, and have ever since left open door to the ladies...."

We have drifted away for the moment from the railroad. I wanted to show, through Mr. Willis's observant eyes, the Northern New York of the day that the Black River & Utica was first being builded. One other excerpt has observed the various sentiments, sacred and profane, penciled about the place and its excellent hotel and concludes:

"... Farther off ... a man records the arrival of himself 'and servant,' below which is the following inscription:

"'G. Squires, wife and two babies. No servant, owing to the hardness of the times.'

"And under this again;

"'G. W. Douglas, and servant. No wife and babies, owing to the hardness of the times.'"

The tremendous popularity of Trenton Falls in those early days was a vast aid to the slender passenger possibilities of the early Black River & Utica. There was not much else for it south of Boonville. True it was that at that thriving village it tapped the fairly busy Black River Canal which led down to the navigable upper waters of that river. Yet this was hardly satisfactory to the progressive folk of the Black River valley. They kept the project alive. And once when the old company's continued existence became quite hopeless they helped effect a complete reorganization of it, under the title of the Utica & Black River. This was formally accomplished, March 31, 1860. As the Utica & Black River, the new railroad came, upon its completion into the North Country, into a season of continued prosperity. It did not share the vast reversals of fortune of its larger competitor, the Rome, Watertown & Ogdensburgh. Through all the years of its complete operation as a separate railroad it never missed its six per cent dividends. It was a delight, both to its owners and to the communities it served.

The Black River road thrust itself into Lowville in the fall of 1868. Four years later it had reached Carthage. The next year it was at the bank of the St. Lawrence, at Clayton. And before the end of the following year it again touched with its rails the shore of that great river; at both Morristown and Ogdensburgh. As railroads went, in those days, it was at last a through-route; with important connections at both of its terminals. At Utica it had fine shop and yard facilities adjoining the tracks of the New York Central & Hudson River Railroad, whose venerable passenger station it shared. And, when at one time, it sought a close personal connection for itself with the Ontario & Western there, it built an expensive bridge connection over the New York Central tracks. This bridge is now gone, but the piers remain.

At both Clayton and Ogdensburgh the Black River road possessed fine waterside terminals. Its station in the latter city still stands; for many years it has been the local storage warehouse of Armour & Co., of Chicago.

In the busy months that the Utica & Black River was building its line up through Jefferson and St. Lawrence counties, a railroad was being builded from it at Carthage down the lower valley of the Black River to Watertown and to Sackett's Harbor. This was distinctly a local enterprise; the Carthage, Watertown & Sackett's Harbor, financed and built almost entirely by Watertownians and retaining its separate corporate existence until but a few years ago. It was inspired not only by the great success of the Rome,

Watertown & Ogdensburgh at that time, but by the quite natural desire of the one really industrial city of the North Country to have competitive railroad service. There have been few times when there were not in Watertown a generous plenty of men who stood ready to put their hands deep into their pockets in order to promote an enterprise whose value seemed so obvious and so genuinely important to the town.

So it was then that the Carthage, Watertown & Sackett's Harbor first came into its existence, there at the extreme end of the sixties; in the very year that Watertown itself was first becoming a city. Its officers and directors as it was first organized were as follows:

President, GEORGE B. PHELPS, Watertown

Secretary and Treasurer, LOTUS INGALLS, Watertown

Engineer, F. A. HINDS, Watertown

Directors

George P. Phelps, Watertown	George A. Bagley, Watertown
Lotus Ingalls, Watertown	Hiram Converse, Watertown
Norris Winslow, Watertown	Theodore Canfield, Sackett's Harbor
Pearson Mundy, Watertown	Walter B. Camp, Sackett's Harbor
L. D. Doolittle, Watertown	David Dexter, Black River
George H. Sherman, Watertown	William N. Coburn, Carthage

Alexander Brown, Carthage

A little later Mr. Hinds was succeeded as the road's Engineer, by L. B. Cook also of Watertown. And eventually Mr. Bagley succeeded Mr. Phelps, as its President, George W. Knowlton, becoming its Vice-President.

To encourage the new line, which it prepared itself to operate, the Utica & Black River made quite a remarkable contract. Shorn of its verbiage it agreed to give the C. W. & S. H. forty per cent of the gross revenue that should arise upon the line. This contract in a very few years arose to bedevil the railroad situation in the North Country. As the paper industry began to expand there, and huge mills to multiply along the lower reaches of the Black River, this contract grew irksome indeed to the U. & B. R. R. Finally it sought to modify its terms, very greatly. The Carthage, Watertown &

Sackett's Harbor, quite naturally refused. "After all," it said, through its President, the late George A. Bagley, "what is a contract but—a contract?"

The Utica road pressed its point. It finally went down to New York and gained a promise from Roswell P. Flower that the agreement would be greatly mollified, if not abrogated. It did seem absurd that a carload of paper moving eighteen miles from Watertown to Carthage and seventy-five from Carthage to Utica should pay forty per cent of its charges to the road upon which it had moved but eighteen miles. Yet, a contract is a contract.

Governor Flower went up to Watertown and put the matter before the officers and directors of the C. W. & S. H. But, led by the stout-hearted Bagley, they refused to move, a single inch.

"I've given my promise," stormed Roswell P. Flower, "that you would do the right thing in this matter. And in New York I am known as a man who always keeps his word."

Bagley said nothing. The meeting ended abruptly—in all the bitterness of disagreement. The Utica & Black River decided upon a master stroke; it would terminate paying its rental, based chiefly on this forty per cent division to its leased road. That would cause trouble. The Carthage, Watertown & Sackett's Harbor was, itself, liable to its bondholders, for the mortgage that they held against it. It would have to pay their interest. Without receiving its rental money from the Black River road it would be hard pressed indeed to meet these coupons. It looked as if it might have to go into receivership, even though at that moment its stock had reached well above par.

The situation was saved for it by a New York banking house, Vermilye & Company, who sent a lawyer up to Watertown who examined the famous contract and pronounced it perfectly valid. The Vermilye's then announced their willingness to advance the C. W. & S. H. the money to meet its interest charges—for an indefinite period. After which the Black River people came down a peg or two and bought the stock and bonds of their leased road, at par. While the city of Watertown and some of its adjoining communities possessed of a sudden and unexpected wealth refunded a portion of their taxes for a year or two.

Mr. Bagley had won his point. He had the reward of a good deed well performed. He had another reward. His salary as President of the Carthage, Watertown & Sackett's Harbor had remained unpaid; for a number of years. He collected back pay from the Black River settlement; for several years at the rate of $15,000 a year.

I have anticipated. We are building the Carthage, Watertown & Sackett's Harbor, not, as yet, operating it. The construction of the line began late in the year of 1870, westward from Carthage, its base of supplies. The road from Watertown to the Harbor—eleven miles—was constructed in the following summer. After a disagreeable fight with the R. W. & O., its main line finally was crossed at grade at Mill Street, closely adjacent to the passenger stations of the two rival roads and, after following the embankment for a mile, once again at Watertown Junction. Its entrance into the Harbor was accomplished over the right-of-way of the former Sackett's Harbor & Ellisburgh, which had been abandoned a decade before. It utilized the old depot there.

George W. Flower, the first Mayor of Watertown, who we have already seen in these pages, had the contract for the building of this section of the line. He rented a locomotive from his competitor and obtained the loan of engineer, Frank W. Smith. For himself, he kept oversight over the progress from the saddle seat of a fine horse that he possessed.

This section of the road was completed and ready for operation early in '74. But because of certain legal complications the Utica & Black River refused to accept it at once. A large celebration had been planned at the Harbor for the Fourth of July that year and rather than disappoint the folk who wanted to go down to it, Mr. Flower took his leased locomotive and hitched behind it a long line of flat contractor's cars, equipped with temporary wooden benches. His improvised excursion train did a good business and he realized a comfortable sum from the haulage of both passengers and freight before the line was turned over to the Utica & Black River for operation.

The first passenger station of that line in Watertown was in a former brick residence in Factory Street, just beyond the junction with Mill. It was small, not overclean and most inconvenient. But a few years later, the U. & B. R. built the handsome passenger station at the Northeast corner of Public Square which for many years now has been the office and headquarters of the Marcy, Buck & Riley Company. Its original brick freight-house nearby—afterwards relieved by the construction of a most substantial stone freight-house at the foot of Court Street—still stands. Back of it a block or so was the round-house. I remember that round-house well. It was a favorite resort of mine through some extremely tender years of youth.

I have not set down the earliest lists of officers of the Utica road. They are not particularly germane to this record. It is, perhaps, enough for it to know that, with the exception of the Carthage, Watertown & Sackett's Harbor—which, as we have just seen, was financed chiefly by the Flowers, the Knowltons, George A. Bagley and George B. Phelps, of Watertown—the U. & B. R. as reorganized, was constructed and managed almost exclusively by Uticans—John Thorn, Isaac Maynard, Theodore Faxon and John Butterfield—and New Yorkers—Robert Lenox Kennedy, John J. Kennedy (who afterwards had a prominent rôle in the early financing of the Canadian Pacific) and others.

Charles Millar was the first Superintendent of the road. He was succeeded, along about 1865, by Hugh Crocker, who a couple of years later was killed while in the cab of a locomotive running between Lyons Falls and Glendale. It was in the season of high water and the Black River was following its usual springtime custom of overflowing the flats of the upper valley. The railroad was fresh and green and young. The water undermined its embankments and sent Crocker's locomotive tumbling over upon its side; and Crocker to his death. J. D. Schultz, who still is residing in Glendale and who is one of the best-known of the pioneers of the old R. W. & O. in his own arms carried young Crocker's body out of the wreck. It was a most pathetic incident. Yet it is a remarkable fact, and one well worth recording here, that in its entire thirty-one years of operation not one passenger was killed while riding upon the Utica & Black River.

The unfortunate Crocker was succeeded by Addison Day, who we already have seen upon the R. W. & O. as an early and distinguished Superintendent. A little later Thomas W. Spencer, who had been the Construction Engineer of the road, replaced Day, and in 1872, J. Fred Maynard, son of Isaac Maynard of Utica, assumed the operating management of the road, first with the title of Superintendent and eventually as its Vice-President and General Manager. He remained in that post through the remainder of the operating existence of the road.

Steadily the Black River sought to improve its service. As it succeeded in so doing it became more and more of a thorn in the side of the R. W. & O. It touched that system at three points only—but they were important points. It was a slightly longer route into Watertown from the New York Central's main stem, but considerably shorter to both Philadelphia—where it crossed the R. W. & O. at a precise right-angle—and Ogdensburgh. At the first of these two last towns it developed an irritating habit of holding its trains until the Rome road train had come, in hopes of luring Ogdensburgh passengers away from it and getting them in to their destination at an earlier hour than they had hoped. Several times it was suggested that the roads pool their interests and work in harmony. For one reason or another this was accomplished but once—the R. W. & O. management almost always opposed such plans. It apparently preferred to play the lone hand.

The Utica & Black River had a very considerable tourist advantage in reaching the St. Lawrence River at Clayton, in the very heart of the Thousand Island district, instead of at Cape Vincent, which was rather remote from the large hotel and cottage sections. It established its own boat connections with the John Thorn, as the flagship of its fleet.

John Thorn's name and personality were again reflected in a fine coal-burning, Schenectady-built locomotive, which also bore his name (the U. & B. R. in those days had a decided penchant for the engines that the Ellises were building at Schenectady). Its motive-power was almost always in the pink of condition, brightly painted like its cars, which bore the same shade of yellow upon their sides that had been borrowed from the Lake Shore & Michigan Southern. Like the R. W. & O., the locomotives were all named. In addition to the John Thorn, there were the Isaac Maynard, the DeWitt C. West (named after a resident of Lowville, who was an early president of the road), the Theodore Faxton, the Fred S. Easton, the Charles Millar, the John Butterfield, the J. F. Maynard, the Ludlow Patton, the A. G. Brower, the Lewis Lawrence, the D. B. Goodwin, and others too. The road at the end of the seventies had a fleet of about twenty locomotives.

There was one time, at least, when the upkeep of the motive power suffered a real shock. I am referring to the noisy way in which the road entered Watertown, by the explosion of the locomotive Charles Millar, No. 4, near the Mill Street crossing there on May 9, 1872. It was one of the few accidents, however, in the entire history of the Utica & Black River. Augustus Unser, better known as "Gus" Unser, of Watertown was at that time engineer of the Millar, which was one of the earliest wood-burners that the road ever possessed—it did not begin the installation of coal grates until 1874. Unser was standing in the cab at the moment of the explosion, talking to Jacob H. Herman—better known as "Jake" Herman—who was at that time conductor on the Rome road.

Without the slightest warning came the explosion. There was a terrific roar and a crash, followed by a rain of small engine parts over a goodly portion of Watertown. Fortunately neither Unser nor Herman were seriously injured. An investigation into the cause of the wreck, which tore the Millar into an unrecognizable mass of metal, failed to develop the cause of the accident. It was generally supposed, however, that the engine-crew had permitted the water in the boiler to fall below the level of the crown-sheet.

Back of the highly developed and independent Utica & Black River of a decade later there stood a pretty well developed human organization. John Thorn was its President; the head and front of its aggressive and alert policy. The full official roster was, in 1882:

>President, JOHN THORN, Utica
>
>Vice-Pres. and Gen'l Man'g'r, J. F. MAYNARD, Utica
>
>Treasurer, ISAAC MAYNARD, Utica
>
>Secretary, W. E. HOPKINS, Utica
>
>Gen'l Supt., E. A. VAN HORNE, Utica
>
>Asst. Supt., H. W. HAMMOND, Utica
>
>Gen. Pass. and Fgt. Agent, THEO. BUTTERFIELD, Utica

>Directors

Robt. L. Kennedy, New York	Edmund A. Graham, Utica
John Thorn, Utica	Theodore S. Sayre, Utica
Abijah J. Williams, Utica	Abram G. Brower, Utica
Isaac Maynard, Utica	Russell Wheeler, Utica
Lewis Lawrence, Utica	J. F. Maynard, Utica
William J. Bacon, Utica	Daniel B. Goodwin, Waterville

>Fred S. Easton, Lowville

The final thrust of the Utica & Black River into the sides of its older competitor, whilst that competitor was still in the anguish of the Sloan administration of its affairs, came in the ferry row up at Ogdensburgh. By 1880 the once-brisk lake trade of that port had fallen to low levels. The fourteen-foot locks of the Welland Canal, between Lakes Ontario and Erie had failed utterly to keep pace with the development of carriers upon the upper Lakes. The steamers that still came to the elaborate piers of the old Northern Railroad at Ogdensburgh—for many years now, the

Ogdensburgh & Lake Champlain—were comparatively small and infrequent. Buffalo was a more popular and a more accessible port. And yet the time had been when the Northern Railroad had had a daily service between Chicago and Ogdensburgh; some fifteen staunch steamers in its fleet.

One most important form of water-borne traffic has always remained at Ogdensburgh, however; the ferry route across the St. Lawrence to Prescott upon the Canadian shore just opposite. Prescott is not only upon the old main line of the Grand Trunk Railway but also has a direct railroad connection with Ottawa by a branch of the Canadian Pacific (formerly the Ottawa and St. Lawrence). The original boat upon this route was a small three-car craft, the Transit, which was owned in Prescott. In the mid-seventies this steamer was supplanted by the staunch steam car-ferry, William Armstrong, whose whistle was reputed to be the loudest and the most awful thing ever heard on inland waters anywhere. The Armstrong speedily became one of the fixtures of Ogdensburgh. Twice she sank, under excessive loading, and twice she was again raised and replaced in service. In 1919 she was sold to a firm of contractors at Trenton, Ont., and she is still in use as a drill-boat in the vicinity of that village. The important ferry at Ogdensburgh still continues, however, under the direction of Edward Dillingham, for many years the Rome road's agent in that city.

To compete with the service that the Armstrong rendered the R. W. & O. at Ogdensburgh, the Utica & Black River along about 1880 put a car-float and tug into a hastily contrived ferry between its station grounds at Morristown, eleven miles up the river from Ogdensburgh and the small Canadian city of Brockville just opposite. Into Brockville came the Canadian Pacific, beginning to feel its oats and pushing its rails rapidly westward each month. That was a better connection than the somewhat longer one of the St. Lawrence & Ottawa, and gradually freight began deserting the old ferry for this new one; with the result that within a year the Armstrong was moved up the river to the Morristown-Brockville crossing, and Ogdensburgh gnashed its teeth in its despair. It appealed to the Rome, Watertown & Ogdensburgh for relief in the situation.

That road was in its most important change of management—the succession of the Parsons' administration to that of Samuel Sloan. Charles Parsons had had his eye upon the Utica & Black River for some time. It was a potential factor of danger within his territory. Suppose that the Vanderbilts should come along and purchase it? That nearly happened twice in the early eighties. There was strong New York Central sympathy and interest in the U. & B. R. It showed itself in an increase of traffic agreements and coöperative working arrangements. The Rome road tried to offset this strengthening alliance of the Utica & Black River by making closer working agreements with the New York, Ontario & Western, which it touched at Rome, at Central Square and at Oswego. But the O. & W. with its wobbly line down over the hills to New York was a far different proposition than the straight main line and the easy grades of the New York Central. It is possible that had the West Shore, which was completed through from New York to Buffalo in the summer of 1883, been successful, it might eventually have succeeded in absorbing the Rome, Watertown & Ogdensburgh; in which case the New York Central certainly would have taken the Utica & Black River, and the competitive system of railroading been assured to the North Country for many years to come. But that possibility was a slight one. The disastrous collapse of the West Shore soon ended it. Yet the Utica road was a constant menace to Charles Parsons. No one knew it better than he. And because he knew, he reached out and absorbed it; within three years of the day that he had first acquired the R. W. & O. He not only guaranteed the $2,100,000 of outstanding U. & B. R. bonds and seven per cent annually upon a $2,100,000 capitalization, but, in order to make assurance doubly sure, he purchased a majority interest of $1,200,000 of Utica & Black River shares and turned them into the steadily strengthening treasury of the Rome, Watertown & Ogdensburgh. The Utica road formally passed into the hands of the Rome road on April 15, 1886. The mere announcement of the transfer was a stunning blow to the North Country. Now Parsons had a real railroad indeed; more than six hundred miles of line—the Utica road had brought him 180 miles of main line track. Now he had over eighty locomotives and an adequate supply of other rolling stock. From the U. & B. R. he received twenty-four locomotives, of a size and type excellent for that day, twenty-six passenger-cars, fourteen baggage-cars and 361 freight cars. But, best of all, he was now kingpin in Northern New York. There was none to dispute his authority, unless you were to regard the tottering Ogdensburgh & Lake Champlain as a real competitor. He was king in a real kingdom. The only prospect that even threatened his monopoly was that the Vanderbilts might sometime take it into their heads to build North into the valleys of the Black River and the St. Lawrence. But that was not likely—not for the moment at any rate. They were too occupied just then in counting the costs of the terrific, even though successful, battle in which they had smashed the West Shore into pulp, to be ready for immediate further adventures. If they should come to war seven or eight years later, Parsons would be ready for them. In the meantime he set out to reorganize and perfect his merged property. He wanted once again to make the Rome, Watertown & Ogdensburgh the best run railroad in the state of New York. And in this he all but completely succeeded.

CHAPTER IX
THE BRISK PARSONS' REGIME

WITH the Black River thoroughly merged into his Rome, Watertown & Ogdensburgh, Parsons began the extremely difficult job of the merging of the personnel of the two lines. Britton, quite naturally, was not to be disturbed. On the contrary, his authority was to be very greatly increased. The U. & B. R. operating forces gave way to his domination. On the other hand, Theodore Butterfield, who was recognized as a traffic man of unusual astuteness and experience, was brought from Utica to Oswego and made General Passenger Agent of the combined property. The shops were merged. Most of the sixty-five workers of the Utica shop were also moved to Oswego; it was retained only for the very lightest sort of repairs.

As soon as the arrangements could be made, the U. & B. R. passenger trains were brought into the R. W. & O. stations at both Watertown and Ogdensburgh; while the time-tables of the combined road were readjusted so as to make Philadelphia, where the two former competing, main lines crossed one another at right angles, a general point of traffic interchange, similar to Richland. Cape Vincent lost, almost in a single hour, the large railroad prestige that it had held for thirty-three long years. To bind it more closely with the Thousand Island resorts, the swift, new steamer, St. Lawrence, had been built at Clayton in the summer of 1883, and at once crowned Queen of the River. Now the St. Lawrence was used in the Clayton-Alexandria Bay service exclusively. For a number of years service was maintained intermittently between the Cape and Alexandria Bay by a small steamer—generally the J. F. Maynard—but after a time even this was abandoned. Until the coming of the motor-car and improved state highways, Cape Vincent was all but marooned from the busier portions of the river.

Clayton gradually was developed into a river gateway of importance. The Golden Age of the Thousand Islands, during the season of huge summer traffic—which lasted for nearly two decades—did not really begin until about 1890. Yet by the mid-eighties it was beginning to blossom forth. The Rome, Watertown & Ogdensburgh of that decade knew the value of advertising. It adopted the four-leaved clover as its emblem—the long stem served very well to carry the attenuated line that ran West from Oswego to Rochester and to Niagara Falls—and made it a famous trade-mark over the entire face of the land. It was emblazoned upon the sides of all its freight-cars. Theodore E. Butterfield, the General Passenger Agent, devised this interesting emblem for it. It was he who also chose the French word, bonheur, for the clover stem. It was, as subsequent events proved, a most fortuitous choice.

Charles Parsons, having merged the two important railroads of Northern New York, was now engaged in rounding out his system as a complete and well-contained unit. For more than a decade the Lake Ontario Shore extension of the R. W. & O. had passed close to the city of Rochester through the then village of Charlotte (now a ward of an enlarged Rochester), and had touched that city only through indifferent connections from Charlotte. Parsons, at Britton's suggestion, decided that the road must have a direct entrance into Rochester; which already was beginning its abounding and wonderful growth. The two men found their opportunity in a small and sickly suburban railroad which ran down the east bank of the Genesee from the northern limits of the city and over which there ran from time to time a small train, propelled by an extremely small locomotive. They easily acquired that road and gradually pushed it well into the heart of the city; to a passenger and freight terminal in State Street, not far from the famed Four Corners. To reach this terminal—upon the West Side of the town—it was necessary to build a very high and tenuous bridge over the deep gorge of the Genesee. This took nearly a year to construct. Injunction proceedings had been brought against the construction of the R. W. & O. into the heart of the city of Rochester. Yet, under the laws of that time, these were ineffective upon the Sabbath day. Parsons took advantage of this technical defect in the statutes, and on a Sabbath day he successfully brought his railroad into its largest city.

In the meantime a fine, old-fashioned, brick residence in State Street had been acquired for a Rochester passenger terminal. To make this building serve as a passenger-station, and be in proper relation to the tracks, it was necessary to change its position upon the tract of land that it occupied. This was successfully done, and, I believe, was the record feat at that time for the moving of a large, brick building. The bridge was completed and the station opened for the regular use of passenger trains in the fall of 1887.

At the same time that the Rome, Watertown & Ogdensburgh was slipping so stealthily into Rochester, it was building two other extensions; neither of them of great length, but each of them of a considerable importance. Away back in 1872 it had leased the Syracuse, Phoenix & New York—a proposed competing line against the Lackawanna between Oswego and Syracuse, which had been organized two or three years before—but the project had been permitted to lie dormant. First it lacked the necessary funds and then Samuel Sloan, quite naturally, could have no enthusiasm over it. Parsons had no compunctions of that sort. The more he could dig into Sloan the better he seemed to like it. Moreover the Syracuse, Phoenix & New York involved very little actual track construction; only some seventeen miles of track from Woodward's to Fulton, which was very little for a thirty-seven mile line. From Woodward's into Syracuse it would use the R. W. & O.'s own rails, put in long before, as the Syracuse Northern, whilst from Fulton into Oswego the Ontario & Western was most glad to sell trackage rights.

The seventeen-mile link was easily laid down; a sort of local summer resort was created at Three River Point upon it, and five passenger trains a day, in each direction, began service over it, between Syracuse and Oswego in the early spring of 1886. In that same summer another extension was also being builded; at the extreme northeastern corner of the property. The Grand Trunk Railway had built a line with very direct and short-distance Montreal connections, down across the international boundary to Massena Springs, in St. Lawrence County—then a spa of considerable repute, but destined to become a few years later, with the development of the St. Lawrence waterpower, an industrial community of great standing in the North Country, second only to Watertown in size and importance. To reach this new line, the R. W. & O. put down thirteen miles of track from its long established terminus at Norwood, and moved that terminal to Massena Springs. The right-of-way for the line was entirely donated by the adjoining propertyholders. For a time it was thought that an important through route would be created through this new gateway, which was opened in March, 1886, but somehow the traffic failed to materialize. And to this day a rail journey from Watertown to Montreal remains a portentous and a fearful thing. Yet the two cities are only about 175 miles apart.

Parsons was, in heart and essence, a master of the strategy of railroad traffic, as well as of railroad construction. Whilst he was making the important link between Norwood and the Grand Trunk terminus at Massena Springs, but thirteen miles distant, he was coquetting with the Central Vermont—in one of its repeated stages of reorganization—for the better development of its lines in connection with the Boston & Maine and the Maine Central through to the Atlantic at Portland. In all of this he was assisted by his two most capable assistants, E. M. Moore, General Freight Agent, and Mr. Butterfield, the General Passenger Agent. Mr. Butterfield we have already seen. He took very good care of the travel necessities of the property. Mr. Moore had been with it for many years. He, too, was a seasoned traffic man. More than this he was a maker of traffic men; from his office came at least two experts in this specialty of railroad salesmanship—H. D. Carter, who rose eventually to be Freight Traffic Manager of the New York Central Lines, and Frank L. Wilson, who is to-day their Division Freight and Passenger Agent at Watertown. Mr. Wilson bears the distinction of being the only officer on the property in the North Country who also was an officer of the old Rome, Watertown & Ogdensburgh. He started his service in Watertown as a messenger-boy for the Dominion Telegraph Company when its office was located in the old Hanford store at the entrance of the Paddock Arcade. Later he began his railroad service with the R. W. & O. as operator at Limerick Station. From that time forward his rise was steady and constant.

I have digressed once again. We left Parsons strengthening a through line from Suspension Bridge to Portland, Maine, through Northern New York and across the White Mountains. As an earnest of his interest in this route he established, almost as soon as he had acquired control of the Rome road, the once-famous White Mountain Express. In an earlier chapter we have seen how the local Watertown management of the road had, some years before, set up a through sleeping-car service in the summers between Watertown and Fabyan's; using its fine old cars, the Ontario and the St. Lawrence for this service.

The White Mountain Express of the Parsons' régime was a far different thing from a mere sleeping-car service. It was a genuine through-train, with Wagner sleeping-cars all the way from Chicago to Portland. It passed over the rails of the R. W. & O. almost entirely by night; and because of the high speed set for it over so many miles of congested single-track, the older engineers refused to run it. The younger men took the gambling chance with it. And while they expected to run off the miserable track that Samuel Sloan had left for Parsons, and which could not be rebuilded in a day or a week or a month or a year, they managed fairly well, although there were one or two times when the accidents to this train were serious affairs indeed.

There comes to my mind even now the dim memories of that nasty wreck at the very beginning of the Parsons' overlordship, when the east-bound White Mountain, traveling at fifty miles an hour, came a terrible cropper at Carlyon (now known as Ashwood), thirty miles west of Charlotte. It was on the evening of the 27th of July, 1883, barely six weeks after Parsons and Britton had taken the management of the road into their hands. The White Mountain, in charge of Conductor E. Garrison, had left Niagara Falls, very heavily laden, and twenty minutes late, at 7:30 p. m., hauled by two of the road's best locomotives. It consisted of a baggage-car, a day-coach and nine sleepers; six of these Wagners, and the other three the company's own cars, the Ontario, the St. Lawrence and the DeKalb.

A fearful wind blowing off the lake had dislodged a recreant box-car from the facing-point siding there at Carlyon and had sent it trundling down toward the oncoming express. In the driving rain the train thrust its nose right into the clumsy thing. Derailment followed. The leading engine, upon which Train Despatcher and Assistant Superintendent W. H. Chauncey was riding, was thrown into the ditch at one side of the track, and the trailing engine into the ditch at the other. Its engineer and fireman were killed instantly. The wreckage piled high. It caught fire and it was with extreme difficulty that the flames were extinguished. In that memorable calamity seventeen lives were lost and forty persons seriously injured. Yet out of it came a definite blessing. Up to that time the air-brake had never been used upon the Rome, Watertown & Ogdensburgh. The Carlyon accident forced its adoption.

I have no mind to linger on the details of disasters such as this; or of the one at Forest Lawn a little later when a suburban passenger-train bound into Rochester was in a fearful rear-end collision with the delayed west-bound White Mountain and more lives were sacrificed. The Rome road, as a rule, had a fairly clean record on wrecks, on disastrous ones at any rate. There was in 1887 a wretched rear-end collision just opposite the passenger depot at Canton, which cost two or three lives and made Conductor Omar A. Hine decide that he had had quite enough of active railroading. And shortly before this there had been a more fortunate, yet decidedly embarrassing affair down on the old Black River near Glenfield; the breaking of a side-rod upon a locomotive which killed the engineer and seriously delayed a distinguished passenger on his way to the Thousand Islands—Grover Cleveland, then President of the United States, was taking his bride for a little outing upon the shores of the St. Lawrence River. A few years later Theodore Roosevelt, in the same post, was to ride up over that nice picturesque stretch of line. Yet was to see far less of it than his predecessor had seen. At Utica he had accepted with avidity the Superintendent's invitation to ride in the engine-cab of his special. He swung himself quickly up into it. Then reached into his pocket, produced a small leather-bound book and had a bully time—reading all the way to Watertown.

One more wreck invites our attention, and then we are done with this forever grewsome side of railroading: This last a spectacular affair, if you please, more so even than that dire business back to Carlyon. The Barnum & Bailey circus was a pretty regular annual visitor to Northern New York in those days. It began coming in 1873 and for more than a quarter of a century thereafter it hardly missed a season—generally playing Oswego (where once the tent blew down, during the afternoon performance, and there was a genuine panic), Watertown and Ogdensburgh. In this particular summer week, the show had gone from Watertown to Gouverneur, where it violated its tradition and abandoned the evening performance in order that it might promptly entrain for the long haul to Montreal where it was due to play upon the morrow.

Going down the steep grade at Clark's Crossing, two miles east of Potsdam, the axle of one of the elephant cars, in one of the sections, broke and the train piled up behind it—a fearful and a curious mass of wreckage. Fortunately the sacrifice of human life was not a feature of this accident. But the loss of animal life was very heavy. Valuable riding horses, trained beasts and many rare and curious animals were killed. Into the annals of Northern New York it all went as a wonderful night. In the glare of great bonfires men and women from many climes and in curious garb stalked solemnly around and whispered alarmedly in tongues strange indeed to Potsdam and its vicinage. Giraffes and elephants and sacred cows found refuge in Mr. Clark's barn. Outside long trenches were dug for the burial of the wreck victims. John O'Sullivan, for forty years station agent at Potsdam, and now resting honorably from his labors, says that it was the worst day that he ever put in.

It was at this wreck that Ben Batchelder, whose name brings many memories to every old R. W. & O. man, finding that his wrecking equipment was entirely inadequate for clearing the miniature mountain range of débris that ran along the track, put the Barnum & Bailey elephants at work clearing it. Under the charge of their keepers these alien animals pulled on huge chains and long ropes and slowly cleared the iron. Yet it was not until late in the afternoon of the following day that the track was fully restored and usable. By that time the children of Montreal had been robbed of that which was their right. And Charles Parsons, in New York, was remarking to his son, that perhaps, a fleet of well-trained elephants would make a good addition to a wrecking crew.

Once again I have digressed. Yet offer no apologies. Parsons did not let the wrecks of the White Mountain discourage him in the operation of the train. On the contrary, he ordered Mr. Britton to proceed with haste to the complete installation of the air-brake—then still a considerable novelty—upon every corner of the road. He steadily bettered the bridges and the track, tore out the old, stub-switches and substituted for them the newest, split-switches, with signal lights. The White Mountain remained; all through his day, and many a day thereafter—even though in the years after Mr. Britton and he were gone from the road, it was to be operated between Buffalo and Syracuse over the main line of the New York Central. And, inasmuch as he was steadily increasing his affiliations with the Ontario & Western, he installed in connection with it and the Wabash, a through train from Chicago to Weehawken (opposite New York); going over the rails of the R. W. & O. from Suspension Bridge to Oswego. This train, running the year round, and also put at a pretty swift schedule, had little reputation for adhering to it. Upon one occasion a commercial traveler bound to Charlotte approaching the old station at "the Bridge" to find out how late "the O. & W." was reported, was astounded when the agent replied "on time." Such a thing had not been known before that winter, or for many winters. And the fact that for a week past it had stormed almost continuously, only compounded the drummer's perplexity.

"How is it—on time?" he stammered.

"This is yesterday's train," was the prompt response. "She's just twenty-four hours late."

Eventually and in the close campaign for railroad economy that came across the land a few years ago, this train, too, was sacrificed. For a time the experiment was tried of sending its through sleeping-car over the main line of the Central from Suspension Bridge to Syracuse on a through train; passing it on from the latter town to the Ontario & Western by way of the old Chenango Valley branch of the West Shore. The experiment lingered for a time and then expired. It is not likely that it will ever be renewed.

By 1888 Parsons had begun to develop a very real railroad, indeed. The Rome, Watertown & Ogdensburgh once again was a power in the land. It had ninety-one locomotives, ninety-one passenger-cars, forty-eight baggage, mail and express cars, and 2302 freight-cars, of one type or another. Parsons, as its President, was assisted by two Vice-Presidents, Clarence S. Day, and his son, Charles Parsons, Jr. Mr. Lawyer still remained Secretary and Treasurer of the road, even though his offices had been moved two years before from Watertown to New York City. At Watertown, the veteran local agent, R. R. Smiley, remained in charge of affairs, with the title of Assistant Secretary of the company. And Mr. Britton was, of course, still its General Manager, at Oswego.

He was really a tremendous man, Hiram M. Britton, in appearance, a big upstanding citizen, red of beard and clear of eye. I have not, as yet, given anything like the proper amount of consideration to his dominating personality. He made a position for himself in North Country railroading that would fairly entitle him to a whole chapter in a book such as this.

Mr. Britton was born in Concord, Mass., November 22, 1831. At that time that little town was almost at the height of its high fame as a literary center.

As a boy he claimed Ralph Waldo Emerson as a friend. The influence that Emerson had upon Britton remained with him all the years of his life.

At seventeen, owing to financial reverses that his father had sustained, young Britton was compelled to leave school and go to work. He found a job on the old Fitchburg as fireman; from that he quickly rose to be engineer and then Master Mechanic. He made his way down into New Jersey and became Superintendent of the New Jersey and North Eastern Railway; after that General Manager of the New Jersey Midland, the portion of the old Oswego Midland to-day embraced by a considerable part of the New York, Susquehanna & Western.... From that last post, in the summer of 1883 to the management of the Rome, Watertown & Ogdensburgh. That position he retained until 1890, when increasing ill-health forced him to relinquish it and travel throughout Europe in a vain effort to regain his strength. The presidencies, both of the Rome road and of one of the Pennsylvania System lines were offered him. He was compelled to refuse both. His strength gradually failed, and in 1893 he died.

HIRAM M. BRITTON
The First General Manager of the Rome, Watertown & Ogdensburgh and a Railroad Genius.

The old R. W. & O. was compelled in its day and generation to assume some pretty hard, human handicaps. But Britton was a mighty asset to it. He loved his work. It was a real and an eternal delight to him to achieve the things that he had set out to do. He was always approachable, obliging and ready to meet all reasonable requests that came within his power; he had the faculty of making friends of those who came in contact with him, and of retaining their friendship. A man's man was Hiram M. Britton, a railroad captain of great alertness, and possessed not only of vast enthusiasm, but also of a wondrous ability for hard work. The hard problems of his job never feazed him. Even the winter snows—forever its bete noire—did not discourage him, not for long, at any rate. He came, as came so many men from outside the borders of the North Country, with something like a contempt for its midwinter storms. Before Britton had been long on the job, however, the line from Potsdam to Watertown was completely blocked for four long days, and he learned that it was all in a day's work when the ticking wires reported two engines and a plow derailed at Pulaski, two more off at Kasoag, and not a train in or out of Watertown for more than thirty hours. At all of which he would relight his pipe and send a few telegrams of real encouragement up and down the line. That is, he sent the telegrams when the wires remained up above the tops of the snow-drifts and the men were using them to hang their coats upon as they shoveled the heavy snow. Ofttimes the wires went down, and once in a while they were deliberately cut—by some harassed and nerve-racked, snow-fighting boss.

That was before the days of the famous Dewey episode at Manila, but the emergency at the moment must have seemed quite as great. At any rate the Gordian knot, translated into a thin thread of copper wire, was cut—not once, but frequently. I myself, in later years, have seen a Superintendent go into our lower yard at Watertown late at night when congestion piled upon congestion, when the zero wind whistled up through the flats from down Sackett's Harbor way, and the evening train up the line nestled somewhere near Massey Street crossing in a hopelessly inert and frozen fashion, and clean up the mess there. Once one of these inbound trains from down the line coming down the long grade into the yard crashed into a snowbound freight there, and split the caboose asunder, as clean a job as if it had been done with a sharp ax. There were six men asleep in the caboose—to say nothing of two in the cab of the oncoming train, and yet no lives were lost. Even though the Watertown Fire Department spent most of the rest of the night putting out the fearful blaze that arose from the wreckage. Corn meal was spread bountifully about atop of the snow, and no one on the flats lacked for pudding the rest of that winter.

Once, in the Britton régime, there had been nearly a week when Watertown was entirely cut off from Richland and the towns to the South of it. A show-troupe, marooned at that junction for seven fearful days, had rigged up a theater in the old depot and there had played Ten Nights in a Barroom, in order to pay its hotel bill. At least so runs the tradition.

The Rome road felt that it owed some obligation to its old, chief town and all the while it kept steadily at its all but hopeless task, although every night the fresh wind blowing down from Canada and across the icy surface of Ontario filled the long miles of railroad cuts and completely erased the sight of the rails. Parsons had bought plows for the road such as it had never seen before—huge Russells and giant rotaries that would cut the snow as with a giant gimlet, and then send it shooting a quarter of a mile off over the country, so that it would not blow back at once into the cuttings. There is a good deal of real technique in this practical science of fighting snow—and a deal of variance as to the proper technique. For instance, in the Rome road they used to place its old-fashioned "wing-plows" ahead of its pushing locomotives, while the Black River line invariably had its plows follow the engine. It claimed for itself the proof of the pudding, in the fact that whereas in blizzard weather the Rome road almost invariably was blocked, the Black River line rarely was. It is but fair to add, however, that the original construction of the R. W. & O. north of Richland was very bad for snow-fighting; there were many miles of shallow cuttings into which the prevailing winds off Lake Ontario could easily pack the soft wet snow. In after years and under New York Central management this primary defect was corrected. And the large expense of the track elevation was quite offset by the great economies in snow-fighting costs that immediately ensued.

Yet try as H. M. Britton might and did try he seemed fated there in the eighties to buck against the worst storms that the North Country had known in more than half a century. That same storm that tied up his main line roundabout Richland—always a snow trouble center—completely paralyzed the Cape Vincent branch. It came as the grand finale to a sequence of particularly severe snowfalls and hard blows. The deficit upon the Cape Vincent branch that winter—I think it was the spring of 1887—rose to an appalling figure. Finally the R. W. & O. gave up the Cape branch as a hopeless proposition and hired a liveryman to carry the mails between Watertown and Cape Vincent, in order that it might not violate its contract with the Postoffice Department.

After the branch had been abandoned a full fortnight, a delegation of citizens from the Cape drove to Watertown and there confronted Britton, who had made an appointment to meet them. They made their little speeches and they were pretty hot little speeches—hot enough to have melted away more than one good-sized drift.

"When are you going to cart that snow off our line?" finally demanded the spokesman of the Cape Vincent folk.

Britton looked at the delegation coolly, and lighted a fresh cigar.

"I am going to let the man that put it there," he said slowly, "take it away."

And he did. It was thirty-two days before a railroad engine entered Cape Vincent from the time that the last one had left it.

The days of that final decade of the Rome, Watertown & Ogdensburgh were, most of them, however, good days indeed. Fondly do the men of that era, getting, alas, fewer each year, speak of the time when the Rome road had its corporate identity and, what meant far more to them, a corporate personality. For the R. W. & O. did have in those last days those elusive qualities, that even the so-called inanimate corporation can sometimes have—a heart and a soul. Yet, in every case, attributes such as these must come from above, from the men in real charge of a property. The courtesy of the ticket-agent, the friendliness of the conductor are the reflection of the courtesy and the friendliness of the men above him. It is enough to say that H. M. Britton was at all times both courteous and friendly. He was a tremendous inspiration to the men with, and below him.

In the doleful days of the Sloan administration the R. W. & O. began to deteriorate in its morale, with a tremendous rapidity. In the days after the coming of Parsons and of Britton it began slowly, but very surely, to regain this quality so precious and so essential to the successful operation of any railroad. The property began to pick up amazingly. At first it was, indeed, a heartbreaking task. As we have seen, at the end of the Sloan régime little but a shell remained of a once proud and prosperous railroad. The road needed ties and rails, bridges, shops, power, rolling-stock—everything. More than these even it needed the future confidence of its employes. It needed men with ideas and men with vision. From its new owners gradually came all of these things.

Yet, before the things material, came the things spiritual, if you will let me put it that way. Britton gained the confidence of his men. He played the game and he played it fairly. And no one knows better when it's being played fairly by the big bosses at headquarters, than does your keen-witted railroader of the rank and file. Perhaps, the best testimony to the bigness of H. M. Britton came not long ago, from one of the men who had worked under him—a veteran engineer, to-day retired and living at his home in St. Lawrence County.

"We didn't get much money, I'll grant you," says this man, "but somehow we didn't seem to need much. And yet, I don't know but what we had as much to live on as we do now. But that didn't make any difference. We were interested in the road and we were all helping to put it in the position that we felt it ought to be in. In those earliest days, you know, our engines used to have a lot of brasswork. We used to spend hours over them, keeping them in shape, polishing them and scrubbing them. And when we had no polishing or scrubbing to do, we'd go down to the yard and just sit in them. They belonged to us. The company may have paid for them, but we owned them."

So was it. "Charley" Vogel running the local freight from Watertown to Norwood, down one day and back the next, in "opposition" to "Than" Peterson used to boast that he could eat his lunch from the running-board of his cleanly engine; which had started her career years before as the Moses Taylor, No. 35. Ed. Geer, his fireman, was as hard a worker as the skipper. This frame of mind was characteristic of all ranks and of all classes. Indeed, the company may have paid for the road, but the men did own it. And they owned it in a sense that cannot easily be understood to-day—in the confusion of national agreements and decisions by the Labor Board out at Chicago and a vast and pathetic multiplicity of red-tape between the railroad worker and his boss.

Take Ben Batchelder: We saw him a moment ago with John O'Sullivan working a thirty-six hour day to clean up a circus wreck just outside of Potsdam. That was Ben Batchelder's way always. Incidentally, it was just one of his days. One time, in midwinter, during a fortnight of constant and heavy snow, when Ben had become Master Mechanic at Watertown, the Despatcher called him on the 'phone and asked for a locomotive to operate a snow-plow. Ben replied that all the locomotives were frozen and that it would be slow work thawing them out, and making them ready for service.

"Then why don't you take them into the house and thaw them out?" shouted the Despatcher.

"There's no roof on the house, and I'm too busy to-day to put one on," was the quick retort.

Faith and loyalty—we did not call it morale in those days, but it was, just the same. Here was Conductor William Schram with a brisk little job, handling the way freight on the old Cape branch: He had just spent three days bringing a big Russell plow through from the Cape to Watertown. On getting into Watertown it was needed to open up the road between that city and Philadelphia. Schram had been on duty three days without rest. Another conductor was called to relieve him. William Schram protested. He said that he did not feel that he could desert the road when it was in a fix.

Three other conductors, well famed in the days of the Parsons' régime of the Rome road, were Andrew Dixon, Tom Cooper and Daniel Eggleston—and a fourth was the well-known Jacob Herman, of Watertown. Jake was a warm personal friend of both Parsons and Britton. Finally, it came to a point where the President would have no other man in charge of his train when he made his inspection trips over the property, and he advanced and protected him in every conceivable way. He insisted even upon Jake accompanying him back and forth from New York on the occasion of his frequent visits into the North Country.

In an earlier chapter I referred to the easy traditions of the long-agos in regard to the passenger receipts from the average American railroad. The R. W. & O. had been no exception to this general rule. Along about 1888 or 1889 Parsons decided that he would make it an exception henceforth. He violated the old traditions and sent "spotters" out upon the passenger trains. As a direct result of their observations some thirteen or fourteen of the oldest men on the line were dropped from its service. Not only this, but several months' pay was withheld from the envelopes of each of them as they were discharged. Just prior to this volcano-like eruption on the part of "the old man" Parsons sent Herman up to Watertown as station master—a position which he has continued to hold until comparatively recent months.

The "stove committees" "joshed" Jake pretty well over his boss's strategy, knowing full well all the while, that if there was one honest conductor on the whole line, it was that selfsame Jacob Herman. Not only honest, but courageous. It was in a slightly earlier era that the road had a good deal of trouble on the Rome branch with what they called "bark peelers"— woodsmen, who would come down out of the forest and in their boisterous fashion make a deal of trouble for the train-crew.

Jake Herman was told off to end that nuisance. It was a regular honest-to-goodness-carry-the-message-to-Garcia sort of a job. Well, Jake got the message through to Garcia. He picked out six brakemen as assistant messengers, any one of whom would have made a real Cornell center-rush. They were the "flower of the flock."

At Richland the gang boarded the evening train down from Watertown. Somewhere between that station and Kasoag they detrained—as a military man might put it. But not in a military fashion. Along the right-of-way Captain Jake and his lieutenants distributed "bark-peelers," with a fair degree of regularity of interval. Up to that time it had been no sinecure, being a conductor or a trainman on the old Rome road. After that it became as easy as running an infant class in a Sunday School.

John D. Tapley was another well known conductor of those days, and so was W. S. Hammond, who afterwards became division superintendent at Carthage. These men were U. & B. R. graduates, and it was but logical that when Hammond came to his promotion reward, it should be upon the corner of the property on which he had been schooled and with which he was most familiar. He was a man of tremendous popularity among his men.

Sometimes these men of the rank and file had their reward. More often they did not. John O'Sullivan's came when in 1890, after a few years of unsuccessful experimentation, General Passenger Agent Butterfield handed him the annual Northern New York Sunday excursion to Ontario Beach (in the outskirts of Rochester) and asked him what he could do with it. O'Sullivan replied that he could make it go. He had watched the success of the road's annual long-distance excursions; to Washington in the spring and to New York in October—this last for a fixed fare of six dollars, for a six or seven hundred mile journey. The excursions ran coaches, parlor-cars, dining-cars and sleeping-cars, and did a land-office business. Northern New York had acquired a taste for railroad travel. O'Sullivan knew this.

"I'll take you on," said he to Mr. Butterfield.

And so he did. For seventeen successive years thereafter he handled the annual Ontario Beach excursion from Potsdam and all its adjoining stations—all the way from Norwood to Watertown—on a one-day trip over some four hundred miles of single-track railroad. The excursion had a vast business—invariably running in several sections, each drawn by two locomotives, and having from fifteen to sixteen cars each. It carried passengers for $2.50 for the round trip. Few Northern New York folk along the road went to bed until it returned, which was always well into the wee small hours of Monday morning. And yet, it was withal, a reasonably orderly crowd. O'Sullivan kept it so. On the handbills which announced it each year appeared these conspicuous words:

"Behave yourself. If you can't behave yourself, don't go."

Yet a practical reward such as this could in truth be handed to but a very few of the road's workers indeed. Yet it continued until the end to command their loyalty. Not even the cruel handling of the property by the predecessors of Parsons could dampen that loyalty. To even attempt to make a list of the hard-working and energetic workers of that day and generation of the eighties would mean a catalogue far larger than this little book. There comes to mind a brilliant list—names some of them to-day still with us, and some of them but affectionate traditions: George Snell, who began by running the Doxtater; Patsy Tobin, who had the old Gardner Colby on the day that she exploded on Harrison Hill, just outside of Canton; Ed. McNiff; William Bavis; Butler (who had started his career toward an engine-cab as blacksmith at DeKalb Junction, trimming for relaying the old iron rails that the section-gangs brought to him); and Superintendent W. S. (Billy) Jones.

Jones was a much-loved officer of the old R. W. & O. He started his railroad career at Sandy Creek, as an operator, receiving his messages with one of the old-fashioned printing-telegraphs. One day Richard Holden, of Watertown, dropped into the Sandy Creek depot and suggested to Jones that he throw the old contraption out of the window—it was forever getting out of order. Jones demurred for a time; then accepted the suggestion. And in a few weeks was one of the best operators on the line, which led presently to his appointment as agent at Ogdensburgh, where he remained until the days of the Parsons' control.

Both Britton and Parsons were constantly on the alert to discover the best available material on their property and Jones was appointed in the mid-eighties to be superintendent of the line east of Watertown, with headquarters at DeKalb. Later he was moved to Watertown and there became one of the fixtures of the town.

I cannot close this chapter of the second golden age of the Rome road without a passing reference to George H. Haselton, who died but a year or two ago. Mr. Haselton was the successor of Griggs of Jackson and of Close, becoming Master Mechanic of the road in 1878, or at about the time its shops were moved from Rome to Oswego. He built in the latter city the engines that were the precursors of the mighty power of to-day. He used great facility in building and rebuilding the early locomotives of the R. W. & O.—in keeping them in service, seemingly forever and a day. In the North Country a locomotive goes in for long service and, in its difficult climate, hard service, too. There still is, or was until very recently at least, a locomotive in service at the plant of the Hannawa Pulp Company at Potsdam, which although ordered by the Union Pacific Railroad from the Taunton Locomotive Works was delivered to the Central Vermont in May, 1869. First named the St. Albans and then the Shelbourne, she was inherited by the Rutland Railroad and then, after many rebuildings turned over by its Ogdensburgh branch (the former Northern Railroad) to the Norwood & St. Lawrence Railroad. Fifty years of service through a stern northland seemed to work little damage to this staunch old settler. She was typical of her kind—old-fashioned built, and with old-fashioned standards of the service to be rendered.

CHAPTER X
IN WHICH RAILROADS MULTIPLY

THE all but defunct Rome, Watertown & Ogdensburgh, of 1880, was not a property to attract any considerable amount of attention from the financiers and big railroaders, who had located themselves in the city of New York. A local and feeding line of but some four hundred miles of trackage—and most of that in an utterly wretched and deplorable condition—it commanded neither the attention nor the respect of the metropolis. The Vanderbilts in their comfortable offices in the still-new Grand Central Depot, snapped their fingers contemptuously at it. They would have but little of it. They did not need it. It fed their prosperous main line anyway. As we have already seen, William H. Vanderbilt had at one time acquired a considerable interest in the Utica & Black River Railroad. Twice he had actually moved toward securing control of that snug little property. It seemed to be a far more logical feeder to the New York Central than the Rome road might ever become. Yet, eventually Mr. Vanderbilt sold his Black River stock.

"I am not going to dissipate my energies in sundries," he then told one of his cronies. "I am going to stick by the main line hereafter."

As I have already intimated if he had succeeded in acquiring the Utica & Black River, there at the beginning of the eighties the entire railroad history of the North Country might have been changed, down to this very day. It was in that uncertain hour that the elaborate but ill-fated West Shore was being built through from New York to Buffalo—a route ten miles shorter than the main line of the New York Central. The West Shore needed feeders, very greatly needed them, and it was having a hard time getting them. Remember too, if you will, that if the Utica & Black River had become the sole Northern New York feeding line of the New York Central, it is entirely probable and consistent that the Rome, Watertown & Ogdensburgh would have been an extremely valuable and essential factor of the West Shore. The greater part of the state of New York would then have been placed upon a competitive railroad basis. Instead of being, as it is to-day, largely upon the monopolistic basis.

The Rome, Watertown & Ogdensburgh of 1890 was an extremely different railroad from the woe-begone and utterly wretched property that had borne that name but a decade earlier. Reorganized, to a large extent rebuilt, it was a reincarnation of the excellent rail highway which the citizens of

Watertown and other communities of the North Country had built for themselves away back there at the beginning of the fifties. Charles Parsons was never a popular figure in Northern New York. He made no efforts toward popularity. Yet simple justice compels the recognition of the fact, that in the rebuilding of the R. W. & O. he accomplished a very large constructive work. He had relaid and reballasted hundreds of miles of main line track and put down not only many miles of sidings but also a considerable quantity of new main line; between Norwood and Massena Springs, between Oswego and Syracuse, between Windsor Beach and Rochester, chief among these extensions. He had built new bridges by the dozens; purchased and rebuilded cars and locomotives by the hundreds. It was almost as if he had built a brand new railroad.

Now—in 1890—he had 643 main line miles of as good a railroad, generally speaking, as one might find in the entire land. The Rome road owned an even hundred locomotives, ninety-eight passenger-cars, thirty-five baggage-cars, and 2609 freight-cars of one type or another. It was a monopoly within its territory. Its busy main-stem stretched all the way from Suspension Bridge (with excellent western connections) to Norwood and Massena Springs (each with excellent eastern connections). It was in a superb strategic position as a competitor for through freight from the interior of the land to the Atlantic seaboard ports—either Boston, or Portland, or Montreal. Parsons was unusually expert in his traffic strategy. Frequently he went so far and dared so much that the line of the four-leaved clover gradually became something of a thorn in the side of some of its larger competitors. Parsons in competitive territory was a rate-smasher. He did not hesitate to put the screws upon the territory wherein his road was a purely monopolistic carrier. There are citizens dwelling in the northern portions of Jefferson county who still remember—and with bitterness in their memories—how he helped put the Keene mines out of business.In an earlier chapter of this book I referred to the large part that James Sterling had played in the upbuilding of this iron industry. After several successive failures the mines had, sometime in the seventies, been put upon a basis, seemingly permanent. Their ore was good—and popular. At the time that Parsons first assumed control of the Rome road, the Keene mines were shipping out from six to eight carloads of hematite daily—to connecting lines at Syracuse, at Sterling and at Charlotte—at an average rate of $1.25 a ton. Parsons advanced the rate to $1.50 a ton, and they quit. They have remained idle ever since; their abandoned shaft-houses melancholy reminders of a vanished enterprise. Yet the ore is still there, in vast quantities; richer than the Messaba and in the opinion of many experts, extending up to and under the St. Lawrence, and into the province of Ontario.

Oddly enough, as Keene quit other mine districts of Northern New York began to open up. It had been known for many years that in the neighborhood of the small village of Harrisville in the north part of Lewis county there were valuable deposits of black, magnetic iron ore. To reach these beds, to open and to develop them had long been the dream of certain North Country men, notably George Gilbert, of Carthage and Joseph Pahud, of Harrisville. As far back as 1866, a line had been surveyed from Carthage to Harrisville, twenty-one miles. Yet, it was not until twenty years later that a standard railroad was put down between these two villages.

In the meantime—to be exact, in the summer of 1869—the so-called "wooden railroad" was built for the ten miles between Carthage and Natural Bridge. Literally this line—its corporate name was the Black River & St. Lawrence Railway Company—had rails hewn and smoothed from maple. It was so very crude that it was doomed to failure from the beginning. Yet its right-of-way served a similar purpose for the Carthage & Adirondack Railroad which was organized in 1883, and which opened its line through to Jayville, thirty miles distant three years later; and on to Bensons Mines in the fall of 1889. A little later it was completed to Newton Falls, its present terminus.

One other small railroad was built out from Carthage a few years later. It deserves at least a paragraph of reference. The quiet old-fashioned North Country village of Copenhagen, situated upon the historic State Road from Utica to Sackett's Harbor, between Lowville and Watertown, had not ceased to regret how the building of the Black River road—which quite naturally had followed the water-level of the river valley—had completely passed it by. Copenhagen also wanted a railroad. It waited for forty years after the completion of the Utica & Black River before its desire was fulfilled. Then, by almost superhuman effort on the part of its citizens, as well as those of Carthage, it built its railroad to that village, eleven miles distant. A former citizen of the town, one Jimmy March, who had won fame and success as a contractor in New York City, bought a second-hand passenger-coach from the Erie Railroad and presented it to the Carthage & Copenhagen. A locomotive was purchased with a few work-cars and a brave but almost hopeless transportation effort begun.

The Carthage & Copenhagen already has ceased to exist. The recent development of the state highways and with them, of the motor-truck and the motor omnibus sealed its fate. In 1917 it was abandoned and its track torn up, for its wartime value in scrap iron: Its little yellow depot at Copenhagen still stands. And upon it, but two or three years ago, there still was affixed the blue and white signs of the telegraph company and the express company. Yet no longer a track led to it; only a half-hidden and weed-grown row of rotting ties, stretching away off in the distance toward Carthage. In truth it has become but a mere mockery of a railroad depot.

The day of the small railroad apparently is gone; its fate sealed. True it is that the little railroad from Norwood to Waddington and the one that the Lewis family built from Lowville to Croghan and Beaver Falls are both still in operation, but these have large local industries to serve—they are, in fact, hardly more than independently operating industrial sidings. So, too, has continued the branch road from Gouverneur to Edwards, which Engineer Bockus helped open in 1893 and upon which he has run ever since.

Charles Parsons had but little use for the small railroad. He thought of railroads in large units indeed. His thought of the Rome, Watertown & Ogdensburgh was, forever and a day, as a trunk-line, nothing less. Sometimes he talked, rather airily to be sure, of buying the Ogdensburgh & Lake Champlain or even the Wabash. Yet, in reality, he would have had nothing of either of these somewhat moribund properties. He did not need them. They were not germane to a single one of his plans. For one, and the most important thing, neither of them could stand alone. The R. W. & O. could. In the largest sense, it was a self-contained property; with its monopolistic control of a huge territory, rich in basic wealth and still in a period of healthy and continued growth.

Once, there at the beginning of the nineties, Grand Trunk made tentative offers for the control of the rebuilded property. It hinted at a willingness to pay par for such an interest. Parsons paid no attention to the offer. Some people said that he was waiting for the Canadian Pacific to come along and buy his road; there have always been plans for international bridges across the St. Lawrence; all the way from Cape Vincent to Morristown.

But even Canadian Pacific was not the big thing in Parsons' mind. I think it may be safely said that from the middle of the eighties he had realized the necessity that would yet confront the Vanderbilts of owning the Rome, Watertown & Ogdensburgh. At that earlier time they were having their hands full with the aftermath of their victorious but terribly costly battle with the West Shore. It would be some years before they would be in a position to go further afield than their own main line territory. But Parsons could wait—wait and upbuild his property. And show his constant independence of the New York Central.

In a hundred different ways he showed this. More than ever he became a thorn in the side of the bigger road. He slashed more through rates—and raised more of the local ones to make good the loss to his treasury. Northern New York groaned, and yet was helpless. Parsons laughed at it. As far as possible he kept out of it. He cut the wires. His right-hand man, Hiram M. Britton, began breaking physically under the pressure and the criticism, finally was forced to leave his desk altogether to seek, vainly, the restoration of his health in Europe.

Mr. E. S. Bowen succeeded Mr. Britton as General Manager of the road. A quiet, gentle sort of a man—a native of Lock Haven, Pa., and a former General Superintendent of the Erie—of far less dominant personality than his predecessor. He came quite too late upon the property to make a large personal impress upon it. The memories that he left of himself are mostly negative. He was thorough, conscientious, apparently seeking to please, in an all but impossible situation. He was the last General Manager of the Rome, Watertown & Ogdensburgh Railroad.

The steadily increasing clamor of the North Country against the road and its management brought a man up from the South with a definite scheme for building a competitive relief line into it. His name was Austin Corbin, and while primarily he was always promoter rather than railroader, he did have one or two railroad successes distinctly to his credit. In control of the Long Island, his had been the vision that planned the creation of a great ocean terminal at Fort Pond Bay, near Montauk Point. From here Corbin saw four-day steamers plying that would connect America and Europe. A day would be saved in not bringing these fast super-craft in and out of the crowded harbor of New York. It was a fascinating plan and one which still is revived every few years.

Corbin did some distinctly creative work upon the Long Island; and yet forever was promoter, rather than railroader. He had associated with himself, A. A. McLeod, who a little later was to achieve a spectacular notoriety by successfully uniting—for a short time—such conservative properties as Reading, Lehigh Valley and Boston & Maine into a single, sprawling, top-heavy railroad. Together these men had picked up for a song an unhappy railroad, which stretched more than halfway across New York State and which was known as the Utica, Ithaca & Elmira. Corbin acquired this road in 1882. It was a wonder. It reached neither Utica nor Ithaca nor Elmira. Starting at Horseheads, four or five miles north of Elmira, it twisted and turned itself through the hills of the Southern Tier and of Central New York, narrowly missing Ithaca—which steadily and consistently refused to build itself up the hill to meet it—threading Cortland and finally terminating at Canastota.

This road came almost as a gift to Corbin and his associates. Its sole value was that in its brief course it intersected nearly all of the important railroads in New York state; the Pennsylvania, Erie, Lehigh Valley, Lackawanna, and the New York Central. Corbin renamed the road, Elmira, Cortland & Northern, and in 1887, extended it north from Canastota to Camden, intersecting the Ontario & Western and the Rome road. He was then within about fifty miles of Watertown. At about the same time he gave his property its own entrance well within the heart of Elmira.

Vainly Corbin tried to peddle this road either to the Pennsylvania or to the Vanderbilts. He finally offered it to them at the assumption of its mortgage-bonds and its fixed charges. Even then it fell dead. As a last resource he determined upon Watertown. Word of that small but growing city's traffic plight had come to him. He jumped aboard a train and went up to the rich county-seat of Jefferson, cultivated the friendship of its men of affairs. Alluringly he spoke to them of the road he owned, of its rare connections, its peculiar value as a coal-carrier, his ambition to thrust it still further across the state.

So there was formed, in May, 1890, the Camden, Watertown & Northern Railroad to fill at least the fifty mile gap between Camden, which was nothing as a railroad terminus, and Watertown, which even then had a heavy originating traffic. Watertown even in 1890, was employing 2500 workers in its factories which alone burned more than 33,000 tons of coal annually. It was receiving 68,000 tons of freight a year and sending out about 178,000. It was a fair fling under any conditions for a competing railroad; under the peculiar conditions that then prevailed seemingly a double opportunity.

Corbin, himself, became President of the Camden, Watertown & Northern. As its Secretary and Treasurer, James L. Newton was chosen. Around these men a most representative directorate was grouped; S. F. Bagg, B. B. Taggart, H. F. Inglehart, George W. Knowlton, George A. Bagley and A. D. Remington. Whatever might have been Corbin's motive in the entire undertaking, there was no mistaking the motives of the Watertown men, who had gathered about him. They were determined to give their town a competing line; to undo, if possible, the fiasco of a few years before when the Carthage, Watertown & Sackett's Harbor had passed from their hands to hands unfriendly and alien.

All these preparations Parsons watched with a great equanimity. He realized the potential weaknesses of the connecting link of the proposed new line; the terrific curves and the heavy grades of the E. C. & N. Perhaps, he realized these fundamental weaknesses all the more because of the steadily growing alliance between his road and the Ontario & Western. The R. W. & O. sought to dig more deeply than ever into the sides of the Vanderbilts by taking more and more traffic away from them; in the five years from 1885 to 1890, the business delivered by the Rome road to the New York Central at Utica, at Rome and at Syracuse had dwindled from two million dollars a year to a little less than a million, and that of the Ontario & Western had practically doubled.

The Vanderbilts have never taken punishment easily. But they are good waiters. And apparently they did not propose in this instance to be hurried into reprisals. William H. Vanderbilt hated to do business with Charles Parsons. He detested going down to the Rome road's offices in Wall Street, and there facing his new rival, a tall, cadaverous man, whose hair in his Rome road years had changed from part-white to snow-white, and who persisted in an inordinate habit of sitting at his desk in his stocking feet; sometimes Parsons flaunted his feet upon the radiator. If the pedal extremities of the fastidious Vanderbilt ever hurt him, he succeeded at least in keeping his shoes on. Decency compels many things.

Across from Parsons sat his son, another Charles, who held the post of Vice-President of the road of which his father was President. Together they smoked cigarettes, incessantly. It was not usual for elderly men in those days to smoke cigarettes and because the elder Parsons did it in his office, Mr. Vanderbilt distrusted him all the more.

And yet, there were about Parsons certain distinct qualities of charm and interest. A State of Maine man—he came from Kennebunkport—he was a born horse-trader, as his operations in the Rome, Watertown & Ogdensburgh steadily showed. He was not a man to pay for that which he might possibly get for nothing. On one memorable occasion he came to the office of William Buchanan, the veteran Motive Power Superintendent of the New York Central, who designed and built the famous No. 999, in order to get some free advice on locomotive equipment. The Rome road then had a rather fair supply of antiquated motive-power—it still was using some of the converted wood-burners of its earliest days—and Parsons wanted to buy, second-hand, some of the older engines of the N. Y. C. & H. R. He argued that his bridges would not permit the purchase of heavy modern locomotives.

But the Central folk argued back that they had scrapped all their light engines, save those that they still needed for certain local and branch-line services. In the long run they drew up plans for locomotives suited to the special necessities of the Rome road and presented Parsons with them. From that time on he came frequently to consult the technical authorities in the Grand Central Depot.

"I have a first-class staff working for me and I don't have to pay it a blessed cent," he would chuckle as he went out of its doors.

The funny part of it all being that the Vanderbilts apparently were perfectly willing that he should make such use of their staff.

Here was Charles Parsons steadily proposing the most disagreeable things to the Vanderbilts. The Lehigh Valley which, like the Lackawanna of a decade before, had begun to tire of the Erie as a sole entrance into the Buffalo gateway, and was building its own line into that important city, was making eyes at the Rome, Watertown & Ogdensburgh. Parsons, still smoking his cigarettes, made eyes back at the Lehigh Valley and its owners, the enormously wealthy Packer family of South Bethlehem, Pennsylvania. Together they slipped into an alliance. For ten years Charles Parsons had coveted an entrance of his own into Buffalo. The Packers wanted to get from Buffalo into the traffic hub of Suspension Bridge. On a competitive basis, neither the existing lines of the New York Central nor of the Erie between those two places were open to them.

The interests of the R. W. & O. and the Lehigh Valley in this situation were identical. It was quite logical therefore that they should get together and form the Buffalo, Thousand Islands & Portland; quite a grand sounding appellation for twenty-four miles of railroad, which was to run from Buffalo to Niagara Falls and Suspension Bridge. Once formed, there in the eventful midsummer of 1890, no time was lost in acquiring the right-of-way for this important railroad link. As a separate corporation it expended something over a million dollars for land and for preliminary grading.

To complete its line it was necessary that it should cross the lines of the then New York Central & Hudson River—not once, but several times. Up to that time the New York Central had generally pursued a pretty broad-gauge policy in permitting other railroads to cross its lines. Even in this instance it granted the necessary permissions, but this time Mr. Parsons went north to the Grand Central Depot and not Mr. Vanderbilt south to Wall Street. Mr. Vanderbilt was quite willing that Mr. Parsons should cross his tracks, when and where it was absolutely necessary, but, of course, Mr. Parsons would reciprocate, if ever the occasion should arise and permit the New York Central to cross the Rome, Watertown & Ogdensburgh tracks, if ever it should become necessary? What is sauce for the goose is sauce for the gander.

What could Mr. Parsons do? Mr. Parsons acceded. Of course. Reciprocal contracts covering all future grade-crossing matters were signed; and duplicate copies of the peace treaty, signed, sealed and delivered. After which work on the Buffalo, Thousand Islands & Portland went ahead quite merrily once more.

It was in December of that same year, 1890, hardly more than six months after Mr. Austin Corbin had made the first of his Queen-of-Sheba visits to Watertown that that brisk community found that it was to have a very special gift in its Christmas stocking. Watertown was not only going to have one new railroad. It was going to have two. Intimations reached it—in that strange but sure way that big business always has of sending out its intimations—that Watertown within the twelvemonth was to be upon the lines of the New York Central. That seemed to be too good to be true. But it was true. Telegraphic confirmation followed upon the heels of mere rumor. The Vanderbilts, tired of shilly-shallying with Parsons and his railroad and of playing second fiddle to Ontario & Western, were going to build their own feeder line into Northern New York. Already, it was organized and named—the Mohawk & St. Lawrence—preliminary surveying parties were already struggling through the deep December drifts.

All the oldtime rage and rivalry between Utica and Rome as to which should be the recognized gateway broke out anew. The jealousies of thirty and forty years before were renewed. Even Herkimer joined the squabble, pushing forward the narrow-gauge line that had been built from her limits north to the little village of Newport and Poland some years before. Finally talk led to promises. Subscription papers were passed. Rome trotted out the terminal grounds and the right-of-way for the Black River & Utica Railroad that had passed her by there before the beginnings of the sixties. Utica met her offers. Yet it seemed as if Rome was to be chosen. The congestion of the New York Central yards in Utica—it was, of course, well before the days of the Barge Canal and the straightening of the Mohawk—made Rome the most practical terminal.

Railroad meetings were again the order of the day throughout the North Country. Carthage vied with Gouverneur and even Cape Vincent, stung to the quick by the neglect of her port by the Parsons' management, joined in the clamor. And Watertown? Watertown was beside herself with enthusiasm. She saw herself as the future railroad capital of the state. Corbin and his local backers were not slow to take advantage of the situation. Adroitly they urged that while the Mohawk & St. Lawrence would approach the city from the southeast and the upper Black River valley, the Camden, Watertown & Northern would reach it from the southwest. They even hinted at the possibilities of a union station. Perhaps, the union station would be big enough to take in a recreant but reformed R. W. & O. And some one hinted that the Canadian Pacific by a series of wondrous bridges was to build into the town from Kingston and the northwest. In the union station of Watertown of a decade hence one was to be able to go in through limited trains-de-luxe to almost any quarter of the land. And this in a town which up to that day, at least, had never seen a dining-car come into its ancient station.

All that winter Watertown ate railroads, slept railroads, dreamed railroads. Surveyors went across back lots and put funny little yellow wooden stakes in the snow drifts, where there had been potato rows the previous summer and the next might see the beginnings of a great railroad yard. Soft-voiced and persuasive young men went before the Common Council and had all manner of permissive ordinances passed without a single word of protest. Plans and routes by the dozen were filed with the County Clerk. A local poetess burst into song in the Times in commemoration of the spirit of the hour.

As I look back upon the printed records of these proceedings, after thirty years, quite dispassionately, it seems to me that there was, after all, an extraordinary vagueness in the plans of these railroad promoters of that strenuous time. The railroad lines ran here and there and everywhere upon the map. But very little real money was expended, either in land or in construction. The promoters, of both of the proposed new railroads, who suddenly had become wondrously accessible to the dear public and its advance agents, the newspaper reporters, were taking very few real steps toward the real construction of a railroad.

Mr. Parsons, stung to the quick apparently by the newfound energy of his friend, Mr. Vanderbilt, retaliated at once by threats of building a line from his southeastern terminal at Utica through the Mohawk valley—even through the narrow impasse of Little Falls—to Rotterdam Junction and the Fitchburg some seventy miles distant. To link Utica with Rome and (by a more direct line, than by the way of Richland), with Oswego and his straight through route to Suspension Bridge would be the next and a comparatively easy step. That done he would at least have a powerful, competitive route, as against the New York Central's, east to Troy and Boston—and for ten months of the year by water down the Hudson to New York. Yet I cannot find any record of Mr. Parsons buying any real estate in the Mohawk valley.

Finally the Camden, Watertown & Northern did buy two plats of land somewhere in the outskirts of Watertown, a fact which was promptly recorded and spread to the four winds. It did more. It began laying track. It laid nearly a hundred feet of unballasted track in the yards of Taggart Brothers' Paper Mill and all Watertown went down in the chilly days at the beginning of March and venerated that little piece of track. It was a precious symbol.

To offset land-buying and track-laying the Vanderbilts sent the flower of their railroad flocks up to see Watertown, to see and be seen, to ask questions and to be interviewed. More maps were filed. One only had to squint one's eyes half closed and see the New York Central feeder following the north side of the river through the town, and the Camden, Watertown & Northern squeezing its way, somehow, along the south side of it. The enthusiasm quickened. A despatch from Utica said that the contractors, their men and their horses were setting up their quarters upon the old Oneida County Fair Grounds. Actual construction of the Mohawk & St. Lawrence was to begin within the fortnight. Watertown braced up and finished the subscription for the purchase of the right-of-way and depot site for the new road through its heart.

And then?

Then—

On the fourteenth day of March, 1891, at one o'clock in the afternoon, a quiet little telegraphic message—unemotional and uninspired, flashed its monotonous way over the railroad wires into the gray old Watertown passenger station back of the Woodruff House. It read, as follows:

OSWEGO, March 14, 1891.

To all Division Superintendents:

The entire road and property of this company has been leased to the New York Central & Hudson River Railroad, and by direction of the President, I have delivered possession to H. Walter Webb, Third Vice-President of that company. Each Superintendent please acknowledge and advise all agents on your division by wire.

(Signed) E. S. BOWEN,
General Manager.

And Watertown?

Poor Watertown!

It was as if a man had touched the tip of a lighted cigar to a tiny, but much distended gas-balloon.

CHAPTER XI
THE COMING OF THE NEW YORK CENTRAL

OUT of the vast wreckage of great hopes and broken ambitions there slowly arose the smoke of a great wrath. Watertown, in particular, smoldered in her anger. Her position was a most uncomfortable one. Her pride had not only been touched but sorely tried. She felt, and truly, that she had helped to shake the bushes while the New York Central got all the plums. It hurt. Her traditional rivals pointed their fingers of fine scorn toward her. Ogdensburgh chuckled with glee. Oswego chortled.

Yet out of her uncomfortable position she was yet to gain much. She was in a position not only to demand but to receive. And because of the inherent power of that position the ranking officers of the New York Central made every effort to placate her. For one of the very few times, if not indeed the only time in his life, Cornelius Vanderbilt—then the ranking head of the family—made public appearance upon the stage of her Opera House, before a great throng of her citizens, who crowded that ample place and sat and stood there with anger in their hearts, but with justice in their minds. They had not appreciated being made dupes. And yet they stood there willing to give the newcomers the square deal. Which spoke whole volumes for their upbringing.

That was a memorable night in the history of Watertown; the evening of March 24, 1891. The meeting at the City Opera House had been hastily arranged. The telegraph wires only that morning had announced the coming of Mr. Vanderbilt, accompanied by Mr. Chauncey M. Depew, his personal friend and adviser and at that time President of the New York Central & Hudson River, as well as a small group of other railroad officers. The party had left New York the preceding evening. All that day it held meetings in the North Country—at Carthage, at Gouverneur, at Potsdam and at Ogdensburgh. To a large extent these meetings were, however, somewhat perfunctory. The real event of that memorable day was the evening meeting at Watertown. In announcing the affair, but a few hours before, the editor of the Times (we suspect Mr. William D. McKinstry's own brilliant hand in the penning of these paragraphs) had said:

"Of course Mr. Depew will be the spokesman of the party. Having had his dinner, which will be at his own expense, he will be in a good mood to meet our citizens, and will, of course, have many pleasant things to say. But we hope he will come no joke on our citizens. With us, this railroad business is no joking matter. It affects us closely; it comes right into our homes, affects our comfort of living and the prosperity of our business enterprises. It puts more or less coal in our fires to warm our homes, according to the price we have to pay for it, and it makes a difference with how we are to be fed and clothed. This new railroad monopoly has the power, if it chooses, to make us the most happy, contented and prosperous people, or the most dejected and discontented.... It is a great power to have and it calls for the utmost consideration in its use...."

So was laid the platform for the evening meeting; fairly and squarely. To it the New York Central officers responded, fairly and squarely. Even the genial Doctor Depew, to whom a speech without a funny story was as a circus without an elephant, respected the real seriousness of the issue. At the beginning he told some funny stories—of course. He alluded playfully to the fact that the citizens of Watertown had met them without a band—referring inferentially to the first official visit of Charles Parsons as President of the Rome, Watertown & Ogdensburgh, upon which occasion the City Band had been engaged and the whole affair given the appearance of a fête. Mr. Depew alluded half jestingly to the demise of the Mohawk & St. Lawrence and then turned seriously to the real kernel of the situation—the inevitable tendency of American railroads toward consolidation into larger single operating units.

The merger of the Utica & Black River into the Rome, Watertown & Ogdensburgh five years before had been in obedience to such a natural law. The R. W. & O. system, reaching only Northern New York, disconnected and not united to the great railroad properties of the country which spread all over the face of the United States, had, partly by reason of its isolation, failed to properly develop the territory that it had set out to serve. It had been hedged in by barriers that it could not surmount.

It was a good speech, filled not only with good intention, but with a deal of economic hard sense. The crowded Opera House listened to it with courtesy, with attention and with applause. But always with a feeling that the deeds of the new management and not their mere words or promises would be the atonement for the indignity that had been heaped upon the town. And the next evening the Times again said editorially:

SNOW FIGHTERS
A Scene in the Richland Yard on Almost Any Zero Day in the Dead of a North Country Winter.

"... Mr. Depew appeared last evening and made the apology which is reported in full in our local columns. He did it nicely. He called it frescoing. Whitewashing is the common name for it when the job is done by less artistic hands. But, by whatever name, it was pleasantly received by an audience which packed the Opera House and a good feeling was created. Mr. Depew ... did not go into any detailed statement of what the new management of the R. W. & O. proposed to do except to make the general statement that they had come to stay; that our interests were mutual; that in building up the prosperity of this section they would be adding to their own prosperity and that they would be one with us in every way. In carrying out this assurance everything else must follow, and therefore it is sufficient and satisfactory to our citizens. They will give the management a good, fair chance to carry out this assurance and wait confidently for acts to take the place of words ..."

That the new management had some real desire to assuage the extremely irritated local situation became evident within the next few days. The members of the Vanderbilt party had had many quiet consultations with the leading men of Watertown and the North Country generally; had noted with great patience and care the many, many transport grievances of the entire territory. And proceeded wherever it was possible to remedy these, at once.

As a first earnest of its desires it tore down the high, unpainted, hemlock fence around the Watertown passenger station. That high-board fence had been an eyesore. It had been far worse than that however. It had been a slap in the face to the average Watertownian who for years past had regarded it as part of his inherent right and privilege to go down to the depot whenever and as often as he pleased, not alone to greet friends or to see them off, but also for the sheer joy of seeing the cars come in and depart. Upon the occasion of the state firemen's convention in the preceding August, the R. W. & O. management caused the ugly fence to be built—as a temporary measure. But the firemen's convention gone and a matter of joyous memory, the fence remained. One might only enter within upon showing one's ticket.

Now, no matter how common and sensible a practice that might be elsewhere, in this broad world, Watertown resented it, as an invasion of personal privilege. It protested to the R. W. & O. management over at Oswego. Its protests were laughed at. The fence remained. The New York Central tore it down ... within a fortnight after it had acquired the road.

I have mentioned this episode in some detail because it is so typical of the fashion that so many railroad managements, and with so much to gain, go blindly ahead neglecting utterly the one great thing essential toward the gaining of their larger ends—public sympathy and public support. Charles Parsons, with everything to gain from Northern New York, scoffed at these great aids, so easily purchased. Vastly bigger than Sloan in most ways, he, nevertheless, shared the contempt of the old genius of the Lackawanna for public opinion. The Vanderbilts rarely have made this mistake with their railroads. I think that it can be put down as one of the great open secrets of their success.

Similarly Parsons had offended Watertown by his treatment of its newly born street railway. It had been planned to extend in a single straight line from the northeastern corner of the city, just beyond Sewall's Island through High, and State, and Court, and Main Streets to the westerly limits of the town, and thence down the populous valley of the Black River through Brownville to the little manufacturing village of Dexter, eight miles distant. In this course it needed to cross the steam railroad tracks four times at grade—all of these within the city limits.

The old R. W. & O had stoutly fought these crossings; using one specious argument after another. The new management of the property said that the crossings could go down as soon as the street railway company could have them manufactured. It kept its word. The street railway went ahead—and thrived; and the steam railroad lost little by its slight competition between Watertown and Brownville.

One other very popular form of grievance still remained—I shall take up the question of the freight and passenger rates at another time—the persistent refusal of the Parsons' administration to install through all-the-year sleeping-car service between Watertown and New York. The Vanderbilts installed that service, also one between Oswego and New York within three weeks of their acquisition of the road. These have remained ever since with the single exception of a short period during the Chicago World's Fair, when the extreme shortage of sleeping-cars induced the headquarters of the New York Central temporarily to withdraw the Watertown cars. A protest from the Northern New York metropolis brought them back—within seven days' time.

The new management did more. It instituted Sunday trains upon the line; also as an all-the-year feature, a travel necessity for which the North Country had cried for years, vainly. It placed parlor-cars upon the principal trains. It shortened the running-time of all of these. It showed in almost every conceivable fashion a real desire to propitiate its public. And for that desire much of the Mohawk & St. Lawrence fiasco was eventually forgiven it.

One other problem—and a passing large one—confronted it; the question of taking proper care of the official personnel of the Rome road. That is always a difficult and delicate question in a merger of large properties.... The Parsons family was taken care of—although in the entire transaction it had taken pretty good care of itself. Arrangements were made to carry its members upon the New York Central pay-rolls for a season, even though they were quickly off and into new enterprises—the New York & New England and South Carolina Railroad—but never again was there to be such a killing as they had had in the Rome, Watertown & Ogdensburgh. Such an opportunity does not arise once in a lifetime; not once in a thousand lifetimes.

The rest of the official roster was to be continued, for the next two or three months at any rate. With great astuteness the Vanderbilts planned to upset the operation of the road, to the least possible degree. It was to keep its name and its individuality as far as was possible. As a matter of operating convenience it was arranged to abolish the auditing offices at Oswego and to have the R. W. & O. agents and conductors make their reports direct to the New York Central headquarters in the Grand Central Station, in New York City. Similarly orders went forth from those headquarters to drop the old name, "Rome, Watertown & Ogdensburgh" from the locomotive tenders and the sides of the passenger-cars. A rather bitter blow that was. With all of its hatred against the property at one time and another, the North Country cherished a real affection for the name. In deference, to which sentiment, the Vanderbilts still clung to it for a number of years; in their advertising and printed matter of every sort. It was necessary, in their opinion, to emblazon "New York Central" upon their newly acquired rolling-stock in order to permit a greater flexibility in its interchange with that they already held. They had not owned the R. W. & O. a fortnight before its eternal shortage of motive-power had been relieved, by the assignment to it of engines No. 316 and No. 414 of the N. Y. C. & H. R. R. And it should not be forgotten that one large reason for all of these orders was the large affection of the Vanderbilt family for the name and the fame of the New York Central. Both have loomed large in their eyes.

The old Rome, Watertown & Ogdensburgh, quickly reorganized in that March-time of 1891, had then as its chief officers the following men:

President, CHARLES PARSONS, New York

First Vice-President, CLARENCE S. DAY, New York

Second Vice-President, CHARLES PARSONS, JR., New York

Third Vice-President, H. WALTER WEBB, New York

Secretary and Treasurer, J. A. LAWYER, New York

Freight Traffic Manager, L. A. EMERSON, New York

Gen. Pass. Agent, THEODORE E. BUTTERFIELD, Oswego

General Manager, E. S. BOWEN, Oswego

Supt. of Transportation, W. W. CURRIER, Oswego

Master Mechanic, GEORGE H. HASELTON, Oswego

Superintendents

W. S. Jones, Watertown   H. W. Hammond, Carthage

I. H. McEwen, Oswego

Mr. Webb, who also was the Third Vice-President of the New York Central & Hudson River, was now, of course, the real guiding head of the property. Well schooled in the Vanderbilt methods of railroad operation, it was his task to begin their introduction into the newly acquired railroad. How well he succeeded can easily be adjudged by the results that were attained. They need no comment by the historian.

To this group of men was given the operation of 643 miles of busy single-track railroad. Prior to the acquisition of the R. W. & O., the New York Central & Hudson River, itself, had only contained some 1420 miles of line, including those which it held on leasehold. The Rome road then had given it upwards of two thousand miles of route line—not to be confused with mere miles of trackage, which would run to a far greater total. The capital stock of the R. W. & O. as shown on its balance-sheet for the year ending June 30, 1890, was $6,230,100, of which $238,243 was still in the company's treasury. Its funded debt came to $12,672,090 (this latter included income bonds, also in the company's treasury). In addition to which there was a profit and loss account of $762,298. Parsons had builded up a real railroad. Always himself short of ready cash he had acquired a habit of dealing in millions—in a day when a million dollars still represented a good deal of money.

The real problem of the new management of the Rome road lay, however, in an immediate readjustment of its rates; particularly its freight rates. The hemlock fence around the Watertown depot, the persecution of the little street railway system of that community, the irritating defects of the passenger service, were in the eyes of the commercial factors of the North Country as nothing compared with the railroad freight tariffs that it was called upon to pay. Charles Parsons, as I have said already, had had no hesitation whatsoever in putting the burden of his income necessities upon his non-competitive territory in order that he might be in a position to slash rates right and left wherever and whenever he was forced to compete.

New York Central control promised a modification of this situation. To a certain extent it accomplished it. Some of the rates were slashed from twenty-five to fifty per cent, and Mr. Parsons lived long enough to see more equitable systems of freight-carrying charges established on the old line. It was only a short time after the New York Central had acquired the Rome road before the huge Solvay Process Company had located themselves on the western limits of Syracuse. Their location there was due primarily to the salt-beds but they also needed great quantities of limestone daily for their products. This the R. W. & O. furnished by means of an attractive low rate. And, after a little time, there was a solid train each day from Chaumont on the old Cape branch to Syracuse, laden exclusively with limestone rock. At other times there would be solid trains of paper, and in the season, of such rare specialties as strawberries from the Richland section and turkeys from St. Lawrence county for the New York City markets. And despite the well-famed superiority of the North Country in cheese making, its rich dairy areas were invaded by the milk-supply companies of the swift-growing metropolis.

All made business—and lots of it—for the new owners of the North Country's old road. They could afford to forget Parsons' dream of a through route along the northerly border of the country—single-track and filled with hard curvature and grades—to the seaboard docks of Portland, Maine. The intensive development of the Rome, Watertown & Ogdensburgh was their opportunity; and this opportunity they promptly seized. And accomplished. Even the once despised Lake Ontario Shore Railroad came at last into its own. Along its rails upgrew the greatest orchard industry in the United States. And even as powerful and as resourceful a railroad as the New York Central, at times, is hard put to find sufficient equipment for the proper handling of the vast quantities of apples, pears and peaches that to-day are grown upon the gentle south shore of Ontario.

The Vanderbilts paid a high price for the R. W. & O. And then it was a bargain. Not only was competition practically forestalled forever in one of the richest industrial and agricultural areas in the entire United States—by an odd coincidence the actual acquisition of the R. W. & O. was followed a few months later by the enactment of a state law forbidding one railroad acquiring a parallel or competing line—but the menace of the powerful and strategic Canadian Pacific ever reaching the city of New York was practically removed. A high price, and yet a low one. Which marks the beginning and the end of railroad strategy.

For some time now we have lost track of Mr. Austin Corbin and his ambitious plan of the Camden, Watertown & Northern. Upon the explosion of the Mohawk & St. Lawrence bubble a good many keen Watertown men who were bent, heart and soul, upon providing their community with competitive railroad service turned earnestly toward the Corbin scheme. The most of the $60,000 that had been hastily subscribed in the town toward providing the Mohawk & St. Lawrence with a free right-of-way and depot grounds through it, was turned over to Mr. Corbin. Edward M. Gates, who was very active in the matter, went further. He wired Mr. H. Walter Webb, who, as Third Vice-President of the New York Central, and personal representative of the Vanderbilts, had made a personal subscription of $30,000 to the Watertown fund, if he, too, would agree to turning his subscription to the Camden, Watertown & Northern. There is no record of a reply from Mr. Webb on this proposition.

Gradually Corbin grew lukewarm upon his Camden, Watertown & Northern plan. Truth to tell, he had lost his largest opportunity on the day that Charles Parsons had landed the Vanderbilts with the Rome, Watertown & Ogdensburgh. They had needed that road. They had never thought that they needed the Elmira, Cortland & Northern, not even at the time that Corbin offered it to them at the assumption of its mortgage-bonds and its fixed charges. Eventually he succeeded in getting the Lehigh Valley, which at just that time was cherishing a fond idea that it might succeed in seriously cutting into the New York Central's traffic between the seaboard and Central and Northern New York, to buy the E. C. & N. Thereafter the Corbin project disappeared. From time to time it has been revived, as a possible extension of the Lehigh Valley, north from its present unsatisfactory terminal at Camden to Watertown or even beyond. It is hardly likely now that that extension will ever be builded. For one thing, the day of building competing railroads is over, and for another, the E. C. & N. is far too unsatisfactory a railroad dog to which to tie an efficient tail. The Ontario & Western would have been a far more advantageous opportunity.

Out of all the tumult and excitement of that strenuous winter of 1890-91 the net result then to Northern New York was no new railroads. No, permit me to correct that statement. One new railroad was builded, and an important enterprise it was. A brother of H. Walter Webb's, Dr. Seward Webb, who had married into the Vanderbilt family, was instrumental in acquiring from Henry S. Ives, of New York, and some of his associates, the little narrow-gauge Herkimer, Newport & Poland Railroad, stretching some twenty miles northward from Herkimer in the Mohawk valley and upon the main line of the New York Central. With the road renamed, the Mohawk & Malone, Dr. Webb conceived the idea of building it through the North Woods to the Canada line. Where the long ago promoters of the Sackett's Harbor & Saratoga had failed, he succeeded after a fashion. He moved the contractors' duffle from the terminal of the nascent Mohawk & St. Lawrence, at Utica, down to Herkimer, and began by first changing the H. N. & P. into a standard-gauge railroad. This done he proceeded with its extension, up the valley of the Canada Creek to Remsen, where it touched the Utica line of the R. W. & O. (the main line of the former Utica & Black River).

This done, and arrangements made for handling the through trains of the Mohawk & Malone over the R. W. & O. for the twenty-two miles between Utica and Remsen, Dr. Webb struck his new road off through the depths of the untrodden forests for nearly 150 miles. At first it was said that it was his aim to meet and terminate his line at Tupper Lake, which had been reached by the one-time Northern Adirondack from Moira, on the Ogdensburgh & Lake Champlain. Dr. Webb did meet this line, also the tenuous branch of the Delaware & Hudson, extending westward from Plattsburg, and then down to Saranac Lake and Lake Placid. But he passed by all of these. His scheme was a far more ambitious one. He had determined to build a railroad from Utica to Montreal, and build a railroad from Utica to Montreal he did. Before he was done the New York Central had its own rails from its main line almost into the very heart of the Canadian metropolis. And while this route was a little longer in mileage between New York City and Montreal than the direct routes along both shores of Lake Champlain, it possessed large strategic value for the western end of the New York Central & Hudson River. And it was entirely a Vanderbilt line. As such it probably was worth all it cost; and it was not a cheap road to build.

This line was then the one tangible result of the most agitated railroad experience that the people of New York state ever faced—with the possible exception of the West Shore fiasco. The other plans—you still can find them by the dozens carefully filed in the clerk's office of the Northern New York counties—all came to nought. The folk of the North Country ceased their dreamings; settled down to the intensive development of their rarely rich territory. And sought to make its existing transport facilities equal to their every need.

CHAPTER XII
THE END OF THE STORY

FOR six or seven years after it had secured possession of the property, the New York Central continued the operation of the Rome, Watertown & Ogdensburgh as a separate railroad, to a very large degree, at least. Gradually, however, the individual executive officers of the leased road ceased to exist; in some cases berths with the parent road were found for them; in others, they were glad to retire to a life of comfortable ease. The separate corporate existence of the R. W. & O. as well as that of the Utica & Black River and the Carthage, Watertown & Sackett's Harbor, was continued, however, until 1914, when the Vanderbilts made a single corporation under the title of the New York Central Railroad of some of their most important properties; the New York Central & Hudson River, the Lake Shore & Michigan Southern and the Rome, Watertown & Ogdensburgh, chief amongst them. That step taken, the R. W. & O. had ceased to exist—legally as well as technically. Yet the work that it had done in the development of a huge community of communities could never die. It was to live after it; for many years to come.

On the 20th of May, 1891, within three months after the leasing of the Rome road, its headquarters were moved back to the place where originally they had been located, and from which they never should have been removed—Watertown. The entire property was then consolidated into a single division, and Mr. McEwen brought over from Oswego to become its Superintendent, with Mr. Jones his assistant at Oswego and Mr. Hammond in a similar capacity at Watertown. Mr. P. E. Crowley was, also, promoted at this time to the position of Chief Despatcher of the division. This arrangement did not long continue, however. Charles Parsons already was interesting himself in the New York & New England, and presently he called to that property, as superintendents, Mr. Bowen and Mr. Jones, who established their offices at Hartford, Conn. Soon afterwards Mr. Hammond followed them. There had come a real change in régime.

The R. W. & O. division of the New York Central & Hudson River, as the old property then became known, stretched all the way from Suspension Bridge to Massena Springs and was, I believe, with its 643 miles of route mileage, the longest single railroad division in the United States at that time. To run that division was a man's job, and only a real man could survive it.

Yet into that grimy old station at Watertown there came, one by one, a succession of as brilliant railroaders as this country has ever known—Van Etten, Russell, Moon, Hustis, Christie. These were men tested and tried before they were sent up into the North Country—it was no place for novices up there. Once there they made good, by both their wits and their energies. Success on that division called for almost superhuman energy. And when once it had been won; when down in the Grand Central they could say that "X—had been to Watertown and made good there," it meant that X—had taken, successfully, the thirty-third degree in modern railroading.

There were a few men between these five, who did not make good—but somehow that was never charged against them. Other jobs were found for them; headquarters felt that perhaps the mistake in some way should rightly be charged against it.

After seventeen years of operation of the R. W. & O. as a single division it was recognized at headquarters that the test was not a fair one; and the famous old road was divided into two divisions, with Watertown Junction as the dividing point and the divisions named, the St. Lawrence and Ontario, with Watertown and Oswego as their respective division headquarters. Just why the system was divided in that way no one seems to know. It would have been more logical to have made the former Rome road, east of Oswego, a single division with headquarters at Watertown, and have split the old Lake Ontario Shore into the main line divisions of the western part of the state. Yet this is history, and not a criticism. The men who have run the New York Central have generally known their business pretty well.

Edgar Van Etten came to the railroad game by way of the historic Erie. He is a native of Port Jervis, New York, a famous old Erie town, and it was just as natural as buttering bread for him to go to work upon that road, rising in quick successive steps, freight conductor, to-day, trainmaster to-morrow—oddly enough there was a little time when he was Superintendent of the Ontario division of the R. W. & O., in the days of the Parsons' control. Then we see him as Superintendent of the Erie at Buffalo, finally General Manager of the Western New York Car Association, in that same busy railroad center. From that task the Vanderbilts picked him for an even greater one—taking that newly merged, single-track 643-mile-division of the R. W. & O., and putting it upon their operating methods and discipline.

Only an Edgar Van Etten could have done the trick. A lion of a man he was in those Watertown days, relentless, indomitable, fearless—yet possessing in his varied nature keen qualities of humor and of human understanding that were tremendous factors in the winning of his success. It was but natural that so keen a talent should have been recognized in his promotion from Watertown to the vastly responsible post of General Superintendent of the New York Central at the Grand Central Station. In those days the position of Operating Vice-President of the property had not been created. Nor was there even a General Manager. The General Superintendent was the big boss who moved the trains and moved them well. If he could not, the Vanderbilts discovered it before they ever made him a big boss.

Mr. Van Etten's final promotion came in his advancement to the post of Vice-President and General Manager of their important Boston & Albany property; a position on that road corresponding to the presidency of almost any other one. Here he remained until 1907, when ill-health caused his retirement from railroading. He moved across the continent to California, where he is to-day an enthusiastic resident of Los Angeles.

E. G. Russell was cast in a somewhat gentler mold than Van Etten. Thorough railroader he was at that, a man of large vision and seeking every opportunity for the advancement of the property that he headed. For remember that in all these years at Watertown these men were virtual General Managers of a goodly property, in everything but actual title. Upon their initiative, upon their ability to make quick decisions—and accurate—in crises, to handle even matters of a goodly size the huge division rose or fell. Theirs was no job for the weakling or the hesitant.

Mr. Russell was neither a weakling nor hesitant. On the contrary he risked much—even the friendship of the organized labor of the road—when he felt that he was right and must go ahead upon the right path. Eventually his policies in regard to labor forced his retirement from the R. W. & O. division. He went, capable railroader that he always was, to Scranton where he became General Superintendent of the Lackawanna. From there he went to one of the roads in lower Canada, and finally to Michigan, where he met his tragic death late at night on a lonely railroad pier in the dead of winter.

After Russell, Dewitt C. Moon; a man with an unusual genius for placating labor and getting the very best results out of it. Mr. Moon succeeded Mr. Russell as Superintendent at Watertown, April 1, 1899, leaving that post September 1, 1902, to become General Manager of the Lake Erie & Western, a Vanderbilt property of the mid-West. He had been schooled in that family of railroads, starting in as telegraph operator on the old

Dunkirk, Allegheny Valley & Pittsburgh, which was gradually merged, first into the Lake Shore and then into the parent reorganized New York Central of to-day. Before that reorganization, he had become General Manager of the former Lake Shore in some respects the very finest of the old Vanderbilt properties—at Cleveland. At Cleveland he still remains, as Assistant to the Vice-President of the New York Central in that important city. He is a railroader of the old school, trained in exquisite thoroughness and with a capacity for detail, not less than marvelous.

Moon's great forte, however, was and still is, coöperation. Men like him. He likes men. A big and genial nature, a quick sympathy and understanding have proved great assets to a railroad executive. These assets Moon has possessed from the beginning. Upon them he had builded—and upgrown.

Still another of this famous quintette to whom the running of a 650 mile railroad division was as but part of a day's work—James H. Hustis. More than any of the three who preceded him Hustis is in every sense a thorough graduate of the Vanderbilt school of railroading. He was born to it. His father, too, was a veteran New York Central man. "Jim" Hustis entered that school in 1878, as office-boy to the late John M. Toucey, then General Superintendent of the New York Central in the old Grand Central depot. He rose rapidly in the ranks, filling several superintendencies in the old parent property before he went to Watertown, in the late summer of 1902.

He left there on October 1, 1906, to assume executive charge of the Boston & Albany. And it was soon after he left that the old division was broken into two parts and the R. W. & O. ceased to exist, even as a division name. Mr. Hustis is to-day President of the Boston & Maine Railroad. He holds the unique distinction of having headed the three most important railroads of New England. After leaving the office of Vice-President and General Manager of the Boston & Albany—as we have already seen the ranking position of that property—he was for a time President of the New York, New Haven & Hartford, before going to his present post with the Boston & Maine. That he is a thorough railroader, hardly needs to be said here—if nothing else said that, the fact that he spent four successful years in full control at Watertown, of itself would tell it.

After Hustis, Cornelius Christie, the last of the executive Superintendents that were to supervise the operation of the Rome, Watertown & Ogdensburgh as a single unit—why the folks down in the Grand Central did not create a general superintendency at Watertown, I never could understand. Christie, a huge six-foot-three man, big both physically and mentally, also was trained in the wondrous Vanderbilt school of railroading. Long service both upon the main line of the Central and the West Shore, equipped him most adequately for the arduous task at Watertown.

It was in Christie's day—in the summer of 1908—that the famous old division was divided into two large parts, as we have already seen; the Ontario and the St. Lawrence. For three years more, Mr. Christie remained at Watertown, as Superintendent of the St. Lawrence, being promoted from that post to a similar one on the busy Hudson River division between Albany and New York. He was succeeded at Watertown by F. E. Williamson, the present General Superintendent of the New York Central at Albany.

At the time Christie became Superintendent of the St. Lawrence Division at Watertown, Frank E. McCormack was set up in a similar job, heading the Ontario Division at Oswego. The genial Frank was R. W. & O. trained and bred. As far back as April 1, 1885, he was working for the property as night operator and pumper, at a salary of $25 a month. Some one must have recognized the real railroader in him, however, for but a year later his "salary" was raised to $30 and the following year he was transferred to the Superintendent's office at Watertown as confidential clerk and operator. From that time on his progress was steady and uninterrupted; despatcher, chief despatcher, trainmaster, and with one or two more intermediate steps, Superintendent.

To attempt even a listing of the able railroad crowd that hovered around the old Watertown depot, in the years that measured the beginnings of the Vanderbilt operation of the old Rome road again, would be quite beyond the province of this little book. H. D. Carter, Frank E. Wilson, George C. Gridley, W. H. Northrop, Clare Hartigan, how the names come trippingly to mind! And how many, many more there are of them.

Yet I cannot close these paragraphs without singling out two of them— Wilgus and Crowley. Here are two more graduates of its hard, hard school, in which the Rome road may hold exceeding pride. Colonel W. J. Wilgus was with the old division for but four years—from 1893 to 1897—but they were years of exceeding activity in the rebuilding of the property; particularly its "double-tracking" and the extremely important job of raising the track-levels for many miles north of Richland so that the eternal enemy of the road—snow—would have a much harder time henceforth in endeavoring to fight it. From that job he went to far bigger ones; such as building the new Grand Central Terminal and installing electric operation on the lines that entered it, digging the Michigan Central tunnel under the river at Detroit and building the new station in that city. These and others.

But none more interesting to him, I dare say, than the task that he laid out overseas in the Great War, building and arranging the rail lines of communication for the American Army in France. A job to which he brought all his experience, his great energy and his rare tact.

And finally, Patrick E. Crowley. Mr. Crowley's connection with the Rome road goes back to the Parsons' régime—even though before that day he had had eleven hard years of experience with the old Erie; in about every conceivable job from station agent to train despatcher. He was with the R. W. & O., however, almost an even year before its acquisition by the New York Central—as train despatcher at Oswego. In May, 1891, he was transferred to Watertown as chief train despatcher and later as train master. His stepping upward has been continuous and earned. To-day as Vice-President, in charge of operation, of the entire New York Central system he is recognized as one of the king-pins of railroad operators of all creation and is the same simple and unassuming gentleman that one found him in the old days at Oswego and Watertown.

That seems to be the mark of the real railroader, always. Ostentation does not get a man very far in the game. In the North Country it got him nowhere, whatsoever. In our land of the great snows and the hard years a very real and simple democracy plus energy and some real knowledge of the problems in hand were the only qualities that put a big boss ahead. Forever—no matter what the name or how long the division—the job up there was the survival of the fittest. The fit man might be here, there, anywhere. He might be a greaser in the round-house, a news-butcher upon the train, an office boy upstairs in the depot headquarters, an operator in a lonely country station. If he was fit he got ahead and got ahead quickly. Merit won its own promotion and generally won it pretty quickly.

Not that everything was always plain sailing. There is one pretty keen railroad executive in the land who remembers his joy at being promoted to Despatcher on the old Rome road. The pay was eighty dollars a month, which was good in those days. He walked into the new job with a plenty of cocksure enthusiasm. The "super" did not like young men with cocksure enthusiasms. He said so, frankly. And in order to drive his ideas home paid the young man the Despatcher's rate for thirty days; then, for the next five or six months at the old-time operator's rate. The young man caught on. He understood. A job's a job and a boss is a boss. And all the jobs in the world are not worth the paper that they are written on, unless the boss wants to make them so. Which may be put down as an unscientific maxim; yet a very true one nevertheless.

Back of these men who sought with all their energy and vigor, of mind and of body alike, steadily to upbuild the old Rome road, was the great wealth, organization and esprit de corps of one of the leading railroad organizations of the world. The Vanderbilts were always thorough sportsmen. They showed it in their reincarnation of the Rome, Watertown & Ogdensburgh. Parsons had been handicapped, forever and a day, by the constant lack of ready cash—there have been few times when the New York Central has been so handicapped. I bear no brief for the Vanderbilts. They have made their mistakes and they have been grievous ones. But they have not often made the mistake of being miserly with their properties. That mistake was not made in Northern New York.

Into the R. W. & O., once they had clinched their title to it, they poured money like water—whenever they could be shown the necessity of such a procedure. New track went down and then new bridges went up—superb structures every one of them—until there no longer were any limitations upon the motive-power for the North Country's rail transport system. A locomotive that could run upon the main line could run practically anywhere upon the Rome road divisions. And when Watertown complained that the traffic was rising to a volume that no longer could be handled upon a single-track basis, the Vanderbilts double-tracked the road—in all of its essential stretches, many, many miles of it all told. They built and rebuilt the round-houses and the shops. "Property improvement" became their slogan.

In such property improvement Watertown has always shared, most liberally. The double-tracking of the old main-stem of the R. W. & O. brought with it as a corollary the construction of a much needed freight cut-off outside the crowded heart of that city. That done the local freight facilities were removed from the old stone freight-house opposite the passenger-station and that staunch old landmark torn down. To replace it a huge freight terminal of the most modern type and worthy of a city of sixty thousand population was erected on a convenient site upon the North side of the river. As a final step in this program of progress the old depot was torn away—without many expressions of regret on the part of the townsfolk—and the present magnificent passenger terminal erected, at a cost of close to a quarter of a million dollars. The management of what Watertown will always know as the "old Rome road" has not been niggardly with its chief town.

Nor has it been niggardly with any other parts of Northern New York territory. Oswego has rejoiced in a new station—the blessed old Lake

Shore Hotel, which for many years housed tavern and railroad offices and passenger depot, combined, is now a thing of memory. Ogdensburgh has a fine new station, and so has Massena Springs. Norwood still worries along with its old depot, but Richland rejoices in a neat but excellent structure, in which the Wright brothers still serve the coffee, the rolls, the sausage and the buckwheat cakes that cannot be excelled. The North Country has never taken to the dining-car habit; perhaps, because it never has had the chance. But it actually likes its old-fashioned way of living; the innate democracy of the American plan hotel and dinner-in-the-middle-of-the-day.

Never can I ride up through it in these fine basking days of peace and of prosperity over its well-maintained railroad without thinking of the days when journeying into the North Country was not a comfortable matter of Pullman cars and swift trains by day and by night; of the days when one came to Utica by stage or by canal and immediately reëmbarked upon another stage for an even hundred miles of rackingly hard riding over an uneven plank-road into Watertown. If one went further toward the North, travel conditions became still worse. Such expeditions were not for tender folk.

And sometimes to-day when I ride north from Watertown upon the railroad—and the cars toil laboriously through Factory Street, as they have been toiling for sixty-five long years past—I press my face against the window and look for a little house upon that Appian Way; the little, old, stone house in which Clarke Rice and William Smith were wont, so long ago, to operate their toy train upon the table and so try to induce the folk of the village to invest their money in a scheme which then seemed so utter chimerical. A house in which a real idea was born forever fascinates me. For it I hold naught by sympathy—and understanding. So many of us are dreamers.... And so few of us may ever live to see the full fruition of our dreams.

APPENDIX A

(Being taken bodily from a poster issued at Watertown in the Summer of 1847.)

WATERTOWN, ROME, AND CAPE-VINCENT RAIL-ROAD

ACCORDING TO NOTICE IN THE JEFFERSON COUNTY PAPERS, the inhabitants of this Town will be speedily called on to complete subscriptions towards the above named Road, sufficient to warrant a commencement.

BY THE CHARTER WE HAVE TILL THE 14TH OF MAY, 1848, to complete subscriptions, and make an expenditure towards the Road.

THE TIME IS SHORT IN WHICH TO DO THIS BUSINESS; therefore it is highly important that every citizen, from the St. Lawrence on the North to the Erie canal on the South—from the highlands on the East to the lake on the West, come forward and spread himself to his full extent for the Road.

TO STIMULATE US TO ACTION LET IT BE BORNE IN MIND that the sun never shone on so glorious a land as lies within the bounds above described. To one who for the first time visits our towns, the scene is enchanting in the extreme. Our climate is bland and salubrious; winters more mild than in any part of New England or southern New York—the atmosphere being softened by the prevalence of southwesterly winds coursing up the Valley of the Mississippi and along the waters of Erie and Ontario, to such degree that for salubrity and comfort we stand almost unrivalled.

WHEAT, CORN, BARLEY, OATS, PEASE, BEANS, BUCKWHEAT, fruit, butter, cheese, pork, beef, horses, sheep, cattle, minerals, lumber, etc., are produced here with a facility that warrants the hand of labor a bountiful return.

WE HAVE WATER POWER ENOUGH TO TURN EVERY SPINDLE in Great Britain and America. In fact we have every thing man could desire on this globe, except a cheap and expeditious method of getting rid of our surplus products and holding communication with the exterior world.

THE WANT OF THIS, PLACES US THIRTY YEARS BEHIND almost every other portion of the State. When we might be first, we suffer ourselves to be last.

CITIZENS! HOW LONG IS THIS STATE OF THINGS TO ENDURE? After having lain dormant until we have acquired the dimensions of a young giant, will we, like the brute beast, ignorant of his powers, be still led captive in the train of our country's prosperity—affording, by our supineness, a foil to set off the triumphs of our more enterprising brethren of the East, the South, and the West?

NO,—FROM THIS MOMENT FORWARD, LET US RESOLVE to cut a passage to the marts of the New World, and, by the abundance of our resources, strike their "Merchant Princes" with admiration and astonishment.

THIS CAN EASILY BE DONE IF UNANIMITY, PERSEVERANCE, and, above all, LIBERALITY, be exhibited. If every farmer owning 100 acres of land, and he not much in debt, will take five shares in the Road, and others in proportion, the decree will go forth that the work is done. Without this, it is feared the whole must be a failure.

VIEWED IN AN ENLIGHTENED MANNER, THERE NEED BE NO hesitation on the part of the owners of the soil. They are the ones to be most essentially benefited. There is no reason why their lands, from having a market and increased price of products, would not be worth fifty to eighty dollars per acre, as is the case in less favored sections, where Rail Roads have been constructed. The very fact that a Road was to be made would add half to the value of land—its completion would more than double the present prices.

A TAX ON THE LAND TEN MILES EACH SIDE OF THE ROAD, to build it, would in three years repay itself, and leave to the present population and their posterity an enduring source of wealth and importance. We lose one hundred thousand dollars annually in the price of butter and cheese alone, when compared with the prices obtained by Lewis and the northerly part of Oneida, simply because they are nearer the Canal and the Rail Road.

BUT TAKING STOCK IS NOT A TAX, IN ANY SENSE OF THE phrase. It is only resolving to purchase a certain amount of property in the Road, which, taking similar investments elsewhere as a sample, will pay interest, or can be at all times sold at par, or at an advance, like other property or evidence of value. The owner of shares can at any time sell out, and have the satisfaction of knowing that he has greatly added to his wealth merely by affording countenance to the project while in embryo.

THE DIRECTORS ARE POWERLESS UNLESS THE PEOPLE RALLY to their aid. They have made efforts abroad for capital to build the Road, by adding to the subscriptions on hand at the time they were chosen. Owing to causes not prejudicial to the character of our enterprise, they have not for the present succeeded. Aid they have been promised, but they are enjoined first to show a larger figure at home. The ability and disposition of our population must be more thoroughly evinced than has yet been the case.

AGENTS ARE AT WORK, OR SPEEDILY WILL BE, ON THE whole length and breadth of the line from Cape Vincent to Rome. A searching operation is to be had. If the Road is a failure, the Directors are determined that it shall not be laid at their door. Let this be remembered, and every one hereafter hold his peace.

CLARKE   RICE,
Secretary W. & R. R. R. Co.

Watertown, Aug. 27, 1847.

APPENDIX B

A List of the Officers and Agents
of the
Rome, Watertown & Ogdensburgh Railroad
(March 22, 1886)

President, CHARLES PARSONS, New York

Vice-President, CLARENCE S. DAY, New York

Secretary and Treasurer, J. A. LAWYER, New York

General Manager, H. M. BRITTON, Oswego

Supt. of Transportation, W. W. CURRIER, Oswego

Gen'l Freight Agent, E. M. MOORE, Oswego

Gen'l Pass. Agt. (Acting), G. C. GRIDLEY, Oswego

Gen'l Baggage Agent, T. M. PETTY, Oswego

Gen'l Road Master, H. A. SMITH, Oswego

Supt. of Motive Power, GEO. H. HASELTON, Oswego

Assistant Superintendents

W. H. Chauncey, Oswego   J. D. Remington, Watertown

W. S. Jones, DeKalb Junction

Agents

Suspension Bridge, G. G. Chauncey
River View, J. B. S. Colt
Lewiston, Samuel Barton
Ransonville, D. C. Hitchcock
Wilson, G. Wadsworth
Newfane, F. S. Coates
Hess Road, C. Sheehan
Somerset, Thomas Malloy
County Line, G. Resseguie

Lyndonville, B. A. Barry
Carlyon, T. A. Newnham
Waterport, A. J. Joslin
Carlton, O. Wiltse
East Carlton, J. C. Wilson
Kendall, J. W. Simkins
East Kendall, George L. Lovejoy
Hamlin, C. S. Snook
East Hamlin, D. W. Dorgan
Parma, L. V. Byer
Greece, W. E. Vrooman
Charlotte, H. N. Woods
Pierces, Chas. Ten Broeck
Webster, F. E. Sadler
Union Hill, C. B. Hart
Lakeside, I. H. Middleton
Ontario, George M. Sabin
Williamson, J. E. Tufts
Sodus, J. P. Canfield
Wallington, E. T. Boyd
Alton, H. S. McIntyre
Rose, A. A. Stearns
Wolcott, W. V. Bidwell
Red Creek, S. G. Murray
Sterling, W. A. Spear
Sterling Valley, W. R. Crockett
Hannibal, A. D. Cowles
Furniss, G. Hollenbeck
Oswego, F. W. Parsons
Oswego, Ticket Agent, T. M. Petty
East Oswego, F. W. Parsons
Scriba, R. M. Russell
New Haven, E. W. Robinson
Mexico, R. E. Barron
Sand Hill, W. K. Mathewson
Pulaski, W. H. Austin
Richland, T. Higham
Holmesville, C. L. Goodrich
Union Square, F. A. Nicholson
Parish, C. J. Lawton
Mallory, R. E. Brown
Central Square, J. P. Tracey
Brewerton, C. R. Rogers

Clay, Wilber Hatch
Woodard, A. J. Eaton
Liverpool, F. Wyker
Syracuse, M. Breen
Syracuse, Ticket Agent, Jennie Kellar
Fulton, F. E. Sutherland
Phoenix, O. C. Breed
Rome, J. Graves
Rome, Ticket Agent, A. G. Roof
Taberg, S. A. Cutler
McConnellsville, G. Gibbons
Camden, H. A. Case
West Camden, D. D. Spear
Williamstown, E. B. Acker
Kasoag, J. A. Frost
Albion, J. Buckley
Sandy Creek, W. J. Stevens
Mannsville, J. G. Clark
Pierrepont Manor, L. V. Evans, Jr.
Adams, D. Fish
Adams Centre, W. H. McIntyre
Rices, Miss L. A. Ayers
Watertown, R. E. Smiley
Watertown, Ticket Agent, Pitt Adams
Sanfords Corners, M. H. Matty
Evans Mills, F. E. Croissant
Philadelphia, C. T. Barr
Antwerp, Geo. H. Haywood
Keenes, W. E. Giffin
Gouverneur, A. F. Coates
Richville, W. D. Hurley
DeKalb Junction, E. G. Webb
Canton, J. H. Bixby
Potsdam, J. O'Sullivan
Norwood, M. R. Stanton
Rensselaer Falls, A. Walker
Heuvelton, H. B. Whittemore
Ogdensburgh, E. Dillingham
Brownville, G. C. Whittemore
Limerick, F. E. Rundell
Chaumont, W. A. Casler
Three Mile Bay, A. H. Dewey
Rosiere, Joseph Burgess

Cape Vincent, I. A. Whittemore

Superintendent of Motive Power, GEO. H. HASELTON, Oswego

In Charge of Repairs

Syracuse, John Knapp   Watertown, B. F. Batchelder

Rome, W. D. Watson

General Road Master, H. A. SMITH, Oswego

Division Road Masters

Suspension Bridge, Geo. Keith   Syracuse, S. Littlefield

Oswego, S. Bishop   Rome, A. M. Hollenbeck

E. Dennison, DeKalb Junction